TIME PLEASE

by

Mikael Curman

www.lightspira.com

Published by LightSpira, Sweden
www.lightspira.com

ISBN 978-91-86613-08-2
First edition, 2012

Swedish original: Äntligen Mogen, 2011 LightSpira

Author: Mikael Curman
www.curmans.se
Bookdesign: Recito Förlag / Förlagsservice.se

© Mikael Curman

TIME PLEASE

business as usual is closing

Table of contents

Introduction 7
MORE is not an option 14
Resistance to change 22
Development by interplay with the surroundings 31
Liberation from the comparison game 39
New opportunities? 69
From words to deeds 98
Epilogue 130
Network and nourishment groups 132
Reference literature 134

Introduction

For a long time I wanted to change the world. Firstly, as a rebellious child - to the annoyance of my parents and teachers – and later as a consultant in strategic planning (Future Orientation and Change Processes) and Work Ethics. Our company's aim was to promote the human dimension of work, to look at profit as a means rather than a goal. It was very much in line with Russell Ackoff´s metaphor, "Profit is for companies what oxygen is for people, it is necessary for survival, but life isn´t about oxygen."

Although a lot of people were thinking along these lines in the 1970s, the business world wasn't ready to accept it as a guiding idea. For example, I remember when working with an insurance company as a consultant how enthusiastic the participants were when it came to visualising themselves as working in the "human company" within five years. They had a lot of interesting ideas, but when it came to implementing them they said, "Well people will only think that we're crazy. And we're earning quite well as it is. So why bother making a risky change? We don´t have to do that." They continued with business as usual. Hopefully, some of their beautiful ideas stayed in their hearts. But I felt more like an entertainer than the change facilitator and world improver I wanted to be. And since I was convinced that in the long run that we would destroy our planet with more of the same, I felt as if I were participating in digging our own grave by continuing as a consultant in strategic planning.

So I moved into working with work ethics with Ludvig Jönsson, a clergyman who was quite well known in Sweden. As a clergyman, he could bring up ethical and existential issues in the business world without having to justify what he was doing in economical terms. A club of CEOs met once a month to discuss issues that were loaded with ethical challenges. A network of change agents of different kinds was formed - business consultants, architects, computer consultants, inventors - who all shared the business aim of improving the quality of (working) life. We held a variety of lectures and seminars. But in 1978 there was an economic depression and companies had to cut costs. Work ethics was one of the first things they thought that they couldn't afford. Ludvig became the Dean of Stockholm and I was without a job for a year.

At the same time I divorced from my first wife. My life lay in ruins around me and I started therapy with an old psychoanalyst. After a year or two she encouraged me to become a therapist, because, "We need more honest therapists among all the word twisters - and don´t say that working with individuals is too trivial!" As a consultant I'd dealt with the big questions - what South Africa should do or the USA. But I'd come to understand that change is brought about by individuals who glow with their passionate belief in what they are doing and thereby impress others who are infected by their enthusiasm.

So in 1981 I started training at the Gestalt Academy of Scandinavia to become a Gestalt psychotherapist. That is also where I met my wife, who a couple of years later took over as head of the academy. For some years after qualifying I felt like a quack in my work as a therapist and thought that I should go back to consulting. But I didn´t want to do that and wondered why.

I found that there was a major difference between the two professions that could hold the answer: As a consultant I had to be very aware of the expectations of the client company. If things didn´t develop in the direction they wanted, in their mind the reason was a bad consultant. So they'd get rid of him and put in another! For a Gestalt therapist the contract is more of a complete process in an I-Thou-relationship, so everything that happens during therapy can be valuable - especially when the client and therapist are on different tracks and have to find out how they will deal with conflict in a constructive and nourishing way. This can create an emotionally loaded moment of meeting.

As a therapist, just being myself openly and honestly could create wonders. And the best results often came when I totally surrendered to the process without trying to push it in a certain direction. Then the important issues would emerge organically. This was paradise for me compared to my life as a much more project orientated consultant.

I also realised that as a consultant I'd had a lot of ambitions for others. I'd wanted to change the world. If I could only convince my client companies of how necessary a transformation was, they would be its best agent. But trying to convince them of how wise I was, and how stupid they were in not seeing the same reality as I did, was not the best basis for a co-creation. As a therapist, I could not tell my clients how they should live their lives.

That was their choice. But I could be of great assistance by accompanying them in their battles with life by making them aware of different decision points and choices, and what feelings and thoughts had brought about their choices or followed as a result. And I could share my perspective and my reactions from what I perceived. But I had to let go of all ambitions for my clients in order to follow the process and making them more and more aware of what was happening, leaving the decisions to them. As soon as I had ambitions for them, I only created resistance.

I realised that the same dynamics were working in companies as with therapy clients - they don´t like others to tell them what to do. So, don´t push the river! It will flow by itself, in the speed and direction that is most natural for it right now.

Although the world may not have been ready for a transformation thirty years ago, it is different now in the face of the threatening climate change. The climate threat has also made us aware of a lot of other planetary boundaries that we have exceeded. So it is not about wanting to any more, it is a necessity. Many people fear that what we are planning to do to stop climate change is too late and too little. We are realising that our earth cannot take MORE of what we have been doing so far. At the same time, we have also begun to ask ourselves if we'll become any happier by acquiring more of what we already have by, "Buying things that we don´t need, for money that we don´t have, to impress on people that we don´t like," as Clive Hamilton put it.

This is a dilemma. Our economy is built for growth. A shrinking economy would cause great social and economic suffering. Maybe we could replace products that tax limited natural resources by immaterial experiences of different kinds in world trade. Or remodel our socio-economic systems.

Much of our present Western culture has its origin in the Age of Enlightenment and its aim of understanding, measuring and mastering nature. We look at living organisms and systems as if they were machines. This makes it possible for us to apply our linear thinking in cause-effect, problem-solution, goal-means ways. And as long as poverty and scarcity ruled our lives, this was quite successful.

As long as we are given problems to solve, or given goals to reach, this strategy is efficient. So our more or less automatic response to the challenge of climate change and the like is to identify the causes of the problems and then try to reduce them. We focus on inventing a more climate-smart technology. This is, of course, very good, and will probably create new business opportunities, but it is also a rather defensive strategy. We have to use a more resource-effective technology to keep what we already have and to create space for developing countries to reach our material standard. They need it, we don´t.

When our basic needs are fulfilled, we don´t become happier or healthier by having MORE of the same. And the earth cannot take more of it. So MORE of the same is not a solution. We have to do SOMETHING ELSE that we can experience as progress and sustainable development. But we don´t quite know what this "something else" is. While scarcity is something we can experience in present reality, all good possibilities are limitless and beyond present awareness. They lie there as potential not yet discovered in the limitless space of opportunities. So fighting the Bad is different kind of art to promoting the Good. The bad things are easily detected, while new good experiences of life are yet to emerge from within and be recognised, agreed upon and defined. In fighting the Bad we can apply the habitual "problem-solution-thinking" whereas finding new good qualities of life to offer at the market requires the co-creation of new goals and measures of progress.

Let us compare our situation to travelling on the Titanic on its way towards the iceberg. Maybe those who say that we have done too little too late to avoid the crash are right. Then some people might say, "Why go tourist class?!" Others might give up and just wait for the unavoidable. And still others may start preparing for a life in the lifeboats. While imagining how life could be there, they might even find new qualities brought about by the change from Titanic´s elegant saloons to the roughness of the lifeboat; some people might appreciate not having to dress up for dinner, others could like the intimacy and human contact or maybe even the heroic physical challenges. So even if the crash against the iceberg were unavoidable, the preparation for a less extravagant life could create some new attractive experiences that can inspire a life after Titanic.

Of course we need to do everything that we can to prevent us from causing a climate change and destroying our common planet Earth in other ways, and at the same time create space for developing countries to develop their material standards. Creating a more energy-smart technology will probably offer a lot of new business opportunities. But only saying "no" to what we don´t want doesn´t arouse much enthusiasm. We also need to aim towards saying "yes" to experience real progress. To find our "yes" and orient towards it, we need new maps of reality to replace those that have guided us so well in fighting scarcity.

The situation the world is facing is not very different from that when people seek psychotherapy: "Something is wrong, but I don´t know what!" or "My present life isn´t satisfactory. I want something else, but I don´t know what." Here my two fields of working experience as a consultant and as a therapist meet. As a consultant I have thought a lot about the need for change, very much in line with what is accepted now in the light of the climate threat. As a Gestalt therapist I have used tools that facilitate awareness and personal change. And as the co-creative part of the necessary transformation requires different kinds of dialogical approaches, I think that we Gestaltists have a lot to offer the forthcoming change process. That is why I want to write this book.

"Time please!" is the announcement of closing time in British pubs. Then the guests have to go somewhere else to continue their evening. It is analogous to our situation on our planet. It´s closing time for more of what we have been doing so far. We have to do something else, without quite knowing what, to continue development in sustainable directions. How do we find out what we want to do instead?

MORE is not an option

At an accelerating speed we have exceeded quite a few planetary boundaries of different kinds. The climate threat is an undeniable visible sign of this. The earth cannot serve us as a stock where we can take what we need for free any more. And we have reached a level where nature's self-regulative capacity is seriously disturbed. I guess that I don´t need to stress this again. There is enough convincing information available.

What is less well known is that more and more research shows that we can neither become happier nor healthier by rising material living standard once our basic needs are fulfilled. Enough is enough.

In his book *Flow* (1993) Mihaly Csikszentmihalyi shows that people´s experience of happiness has very little to do with what happens to them in relation to money and power. It is more about an attitude to life. The research team asked thousands of people from different cultures around the world about when they felt especially happy. The answers, independent of age, profession or cultural background, indicated that it was about an ability to feel joy and a sense of presence, here and now, in the actual situation. This sounds very much like what is today called "mindfulness". To meet *what is* with open senses and an open heart - without being kidnapped by wishful thinking or catastrophic fantasies or ideas of what should be instead. And this is an ability that you can train.

Richard Wilkinson and Kate Pickett, two professors of epidemiology, found that when the basic material needs are satisfied - enough food, clean water, possibilities to keep warm - additional economic welfare adds nothing to neither health nor happiness. Their findings are based on solid research, their own and others, reported in their book *The Spirit Level - Why Equality is Better for Everyone* (2010).

For thousands of years the best way of improving the quality of human life was to raise material living standards. When scarcity is no longer the main issue, the need for economic growth as such is completed, but there may be other reasons for the need for growth. Wilkinson and Pickett found that for the poorest countries, the curves of life expectancy and happiness raised dramatically with increasing BNP/person - but at a certain level, around Mexico, Croatia, Latvia, Malaysia, Libya and Romania, the curves levelled out, so that more economic welfare added very little, if anything, to health and happiness. They found the same correlation between material standard and different measures of health and well-being and its opposites (www.equalitytrust.org.uk).

So, above a satisfactory income level a further income raise adds nothing to the quality of life. Instead, Wilkinson and Pickett found another factor that was crucial for the sense of both personal and social well-being, namely equality - measured as the income gap between the 20% richest and the 20% poorest inhabitants of a country.

They found that health and social problems are closely related to income inequality. And this is valid regardless of the national average income among the rich countries (including the European countries, Australia and New Zealand, Japan, Canada and the USA). This means that the higher the inequality in a country is, the worse health and social problems it has - and the more equal a society is, the better the health and social situation. But inequality between countries doesn't matter very much.

What seems to matter in the rich countries is not your actual income level and living standard, but how you compare with other people in the same society. When people lack money for essentials such as food, it is usually a reflection of the strength of their desire to live up to the prevailing standards. So you might find it more important to have a proper car or the "right" mobile phone than to eat well.

Despite our rising material living standards, people in many rich countries have experienced substantial rises in anxiety and depression. But since these rises seem to have started well before the increases in inequality during the last quarter of the twentieth century, they cannot have been triggered by inequality. (Maybe the causal relation is in the other direction and rising anxiety and depression has triggered higher levels of inequality as a kind of compensation where people try to lessen their anxiety by more consumption.)

Anyway, Wilkinson and Pickett identified some other factors in modern society that could trigger anxiety and depression: Positive thinking urges us to raise our self-esteem. For some of us, this results in a boosted ego accompanied by a narcissistic defence of an insecure self-image. A lot of comparisons, judgemental evaluations and conditional love trigger our fear of low status and loss of friends. We must not disappoint others. Shame (and pride) is the result of internalising how we imagine others see us. If we fear others will see us as inferior, shame is easily triggered.

In the past we lived in small communities where people knew each other their whole lives. Our identity was clear. But nowadays we move around and live in a mass society where we can be forgotten and lost in anonymity unless we make an impression on others.

Inequality increases all these evaluation anxieties. When we don´t know each other, and don´t see each other as equal human beings, we tend to give more importance to the symbols that position us in the status hierarchy.

After having ranked the countries in order of equality, Wilkinson and Pickett collected internationally comparable data on health and as many social problems as they could find relevant figures for in the rich countries. This included:
- Level of trust
- Mental illness (including drug and alcohol addiction)
- Life expectancy and infant mortality
- Obesity
- Children´s educational performance
- Teenage births
- Homicides
- Imprisonment rates
- Social mobility

The results were clear. On basically every scale Japan and the Scandinavian countries (those that are the most equal countries) ranked well, while the most unequal countries, the very rich USA and the poorer Portugal, ranked badly. The result that equality is the crucial factor was so evident that the researchers were tempted to call their book *Evidence-based Politics* in accordance with "evidence-based medicine".

In the light of these findings it seems sad and stupid for us in Sweden to destroy our fruitful equality by comparing the salaries we pay to our top managers with those paid by American (or German or British) giant companies. If we are aware of our comparably high quality of life, are that many gifted people really willing to leave the country for a higher salary? Although inequalities between countries didn´t mean very much in Wilkinson`s and Pickett´s study, comparisons with colleagues in other countries are more difficult to avoid in a global economy within multinational companies. This was what happened when the Swedish energy-company Vattenfall, in its fusion with a German company, had to accept the very generous conditions for managers prevailing in the much more unequal Germany, which was quite upsetting for the Swedish managers who wanted the same conditions. This triggered a debate on how to avoid an already exaggerated race for higher bonuses and salaries for top management. Accepting these superficial material measures of personal value triggers greediness and inequality and moves evolution backwards towards the values of the nouveau riche.

Consumption above a level where we feel that our basic needs are secured is socially conditioned. It has very little to do with material needs, but acts as a status marker. We more or less consciously agree to use certain products or phenomena as measures of personal value. And as soon as we assign a symbolic value to something, it often becomes a goal in itself - like when the trademark becomes more important than the product itself, or when an academic degree is more important than the knowledge it imparts. Certain concepts become fashionable in the business world, such as "coaching" or "mindfulness". Somebody sees an opportunity and starts certifying coaches or starts diploma courses in mindfulness. And even Gestalt therapists, who have had many years of training in I-Thou-relationship (coaching) and mindfulness/presence in their basic education since 1950, train to get a certificate or diploma, because their target groups have accepted these as a sign of quality. What is written on your business card may be more important than what you do or know in reality. How often you are seen in the media with the "beautiful people", if you are recognised as a regular at a fashionable restaurant and the like, might become more important than real friendship and close relationships. You have probably seen many examples of how we move away from the real world into the symbolic world in this comparison game. This happens when symbols lose contact with what they originally symbolised and become goals in their own right.

Having recognised equality as the most crucial factor for both personal and social well-being, it is important to be aware of its real value before it drifts away into the symbolic world and becomes a goal unto itself. At least in Sweden, where equality since long has been an honoured concept, we see examples of this. There is inflation in work titles. Everybody becomes a manager. And at the age of thirty you can become a senior manager. A goal for the government some twenty years ago was to have a certain quota of the population holding an academic degree, but to make that available for many enough of the students, they had to lower academic standards, thereby draining the exam of its original knowledge content.

In his book *Tomhetens Triumf* (*The Triumph of Nothingness* 2006) Mats Alvesson showed how MORE in the end of this drift into the symbolic world adds up to nothing. As more and more people can get more and more of these desired symbolic values, they lose their comparison value. It is like asking everybody in a crowd to stand on the tips of their toes to be seen better.

So where Wilkinson and Pickett see equality as the Gordian knot to be cut for a better society, it is important not to lose track of what characteristics of equality makes it so crucial for a sense of well-being. I think it is about seeing each other and respecting each other as valuable human beings of different kinds. Where the skill of a carpenter is looked upon as having as much worth as the knowledge of a university graduate or as the healing compassion of a nurse. Where we all contribute to the common good with our different specialities. And where we are interested in each other as human beings with our different needs and preferences and yet we are still so similar to each other.

MORE of what we already have or do will lead to nothing. So having come to the end of what higher material living standards can offer us, we are the first generation obliged to find other ways of improving the real quality of life.

But leaving the old and well-known to move to territories that we have not visited before is not an easy task. Our prevailing maps of reality are designed to guide us in our struggle to defeat scarcity and poverty. In our affluent and over-consuming societies we need new maps that are better suited to guide us towards new measures of progress. And the construction of new maps, requires some kind of dialogical approach which contains very much of I-Thou-relationship and other characteristics that make equality such a crucial factor for our sense of well-being. So our common efforts in orienting ourselves in new directions might also help us to develop new tools for living together in a more fruitful and rewarding way where fear is replaced by love and where the pulling force of "yes" is at least as strong as the repelling force of "no". The experiences of the search process might be part of the new goals of sustainable development.

Resistance to change

To let go of old maps and guiding principles that have served us so well for so long is not easily done. We have developed habits that give everyday life routines and meaning. We know how society is organised, where to go in different situations and what responses we can expect. We have developed suitable tools with which to handle our needs, and have acquired the skills needed to use them in today´s society. Daily life is safe and predictable. To leave this behind can be scary. We need to be motivated to abandon the familiar and take a step into the unknown. We need to believe that this step into adventure is either worthwhile or necessary.

We can see this dilemma manifested in the polarised positions of people in their reactions to the present situation. Some people welcome the climate threat as an incitement to change. They have since long been worried about humanity's insatiable greediness and ruthless exploitation of nature. And they are tired of shallowness ruling much of the interchange between people and long for personal contact on a more profound level. They can point towards the climate threat as an obvious, measurable and undeniable manifestation of the need to change, whether we want to or not.

Another group of people have been very successful in society and enjoy what it gives them. They don´t want to change anything at all, and instead view all proposals of fundamental change as being a threat to the foundation of their success. From being in demand, honoured and respected, their skills and manners might begin to be regarded as obsolete and destructive. Of course, this is a horror for them, making them resistant to any change in that direction. So this group tries to deny the evidence of the threat to our climate, and in some cases sees it as part of a political conspiracy. As long as these two groups don´t talk to each other, they can be prejudiced and suspicious of each other's motives. There are also groups of consultants, journalists, authors and other social critics who make a living working for change. Those who see themselves as bearers of stability, and safe survival strategies, can view the change agents as destructive threats to what they have spent a long time building.

The maps of reality, the socio-economic systems and organisations, and our project-oriented thinking in terms of goal-means that we developed in our struggle against scarcity have been very successful. Technological and economic progress has been, and still is, enormous. Our scientific thinking has liberated us from superstition and the authoritarian grip of the church. Education for all has liberated us from patriarchal and feudal systems and promoted democracy. Large scale technology, supported by information technology, has lead to globalisation. The well being of the earth has become the responsibility of us all. The whole world is interconnected in complex systems where changes in one part can very quickly spread to other parts. To impose change on this complicated network can be seen as too hazardous.

But not everything has to change. For all societal challenges that can be described as defined problems to solve, or goals to reach, the usual tools are appropriate, for example, when it comes to meeting our basic material needs. Or in developing and spreading new climate-smart technology. The area where change is most needed is around socially motivated consumption, where it is more about quality than quantity, relationships and experiences more than material needs. Where the main reason we consume more of what we already have is because we lack direct access to the real human qualities that we long for. As long as we fail to express these clearly enough, we let a symbolic measure or an "instead of" goal represent the desired value. So in spite of our experience, we need to find new ways with which to deal with these kinds of issues, yet we stick to the ones we are used to. Why?

By machine-thinking we become servants of our tools

When we have well defined goals, we can construct convenient hierarchies of goal-means or goal-subgoals where one leads to another. Where this is the case, we can often mechanise and automatise the whole process. This is the basis of the industrial society, where the skills of different craftsmen can be transformed into machines. The advantage of a machine is that it doesn´t get tired or lose its temper; it can repeat the same piece of work in exactly the same way time and again. It only does what it is programmed to do - all of which makes it predictable and reliable. The user is primarily interested in the outcome, and usually doesn´t want to bother too much about the technical details of how the machine works. Therefore, to make the machine user-friendly, as much as possible is automatised, and the user only has to learn which buttons to press. What happens between input and output can be left to specialists, who can repair the machine when necessary.

There are good and bad sides to this. The good is that the less that is left to different users to control, the less we will hear about accidents caused by the "human factor". The bad is that the more that humans have to submit to the conditions of technology, the more they become servants to the machines and routines rather than being their masters. The more we are dependent on structures and systems that we don't understand very well, the more we are busy keeping them alive without questioning their purpose. Although they were designed for a specific purpose, we fail to change them when that purpose is fulfilled or changed, because we are too afraid of destroying the ground we stand on. As this organisation of labour in hierarchies of goal-subgoals has been so efficient in industry, it has also influenced much of society as a whole. When it comes to how we organise our socio-economic systems in this form, we are stuck and say, "The system demands ..."

In this way, the form tends to become more important than the content and the aims. What the tools can produce becomes more important than what we really want. It's the dominance of the possible, or as Abraham Maslow[1] put it, "When the only tool you have is a hammer you tend to see every problem as a nail". Instead of studying the issues we find the most important in order to invent new tools for dealing with them, we often direct our efforts towards issues for which we already have tools or research methods available. Objectives that are measurable attract more attention than goals that are more important but intangible. Readymade tools tempt us to do more of what we have been doing.

---

1 Abraham Maslow, *The Psychology of Science*, 1966.

And instead of focusing on the ethical and philosophical considerations of what we have been doing so far, we concentrate on learning how to use the tools as part of being educated in different professions. Rather than learning how to meet reality as it is with whom we are, we learn the maps of reality and are trained to deal with the "map-world".

Living organisations

But today's companies are not very machine-like. They are much more like living organisms. While machines produce repetitive and predictable results, living organisms do not. You only have to think about a plant to notice how personal it can be in its response to exactly the same treatment that you give to another plant. And how many different parameters it can react to, such as temperature, humidity, quality of the soil, frequency of watering and maybe even the mood of the caregiver. So imagine what it is to coordinate a bunch of people in a company. People with their own personalities, backgrounds, habits, preferences and motives for working in that company. A company that is quite often working in a global market, in an interwoven and rapidly changing world of different cultures, needs and various conditions. To make all this function requires skills other than what are needed to master a machine. As long as people were willing to submit to authoritarian leaders in exchange for safe membership of some sort of a clan, it was possible to lead by discipline and bureaucratic rules. But in modern democracies people want to think for themselves and to have a say in decision making.

And in times when we have to leave behind old-fashioned maps of reality to design new ones better suited for modern society, we need to make use of all involved perspectives. Our challenge is to formulate new goals and agree on new measures of progress. In this process we can't rely mainly on hints from the outside any more, but have to listen to our inner voice. We have to move forward step by step in open dialogue. And this is something that we are not very well trained for. At school, at least in Sweden, we are asked for the correct answers to the questions that the teachers find relevant, and that relevance is mostly in line with the prevailing maps of reality. The children's curiosity, reflections, emotional reactions and new perspectives are seldom taken into account. Later at work our job is to realise and be loyal to the objectives set by managers. All this is a training in linear thinking in goal-means, problem-solution, which is the opposite of what is required when we leave outdated stepping stones to look for new paths leading to more fruitful but not yet identified parts of the terrain. Here our challenge is much more to identify and formulate interesting and relevant questions, rather than to answer existing questions. Although habitual, quantitative, hypothesis proving research is often more valued and preferred in present society, we need much more qualitative research for the required transformation.

In 1983 Hans Zetterberg and his research team sorted the Swedish population into three groups according to their focus in life. Thirty-four per cent were "inner-directed", listening to their inner voice, with their focus on "self-actualisation". Forty-three per cent were more "outer-directed" and focused on their appearance in the eyes of others. Twenty-three per cent were focused on survival and the basic needs that ruled the old peasantry. So only one third of the population is interested in creating new values and new possibilities, while the rest is busier adapting to their basic needs or the expectations of others. This may explain some of the polarisation between those who easily accept the need for social transformation and are ready to work for it and those who try to deny the need and want to avoid change.

Neuropsychological aspects of changing habits

We often talk about the strength of habits. One reason why our habits have such a strong grip on our behaviour is that a fundamental change in attitude actually requires a neuro-psychological rewiring of the brain. By modern tools of computer tomography (fMRI, PET) we can see what happens in different parts of the brain while we are coping with different kinds of changing situations. This research[2] enables us to draw conclusions that are relevant to how we deal with the present need for a fundamental transformation of society.

Habitual responses to different situations, like survival reflexes, are more or less subconsciously governed by the "old reptile brain". New thinking, on the other hand, requires a much more energy-consuming engagement from the frontal lobes of the neocortex. To economise on precious brainpower, the brain tries to routinise as much as possible of our everyday life. In order to stay in the lower reflexive structures, the brain tries to resist new impressions that threaten habitual routines for as long as possible, before it lets them in, initiating adaptation and rewiring the brain. If we are too resistant, and try to solve our problems with more of the same, we risk worsening the problems like a compulsory neurotic washing his hands over and over again in his fear of germs.

If we try to persuade or convince people, they will only defend their present position. New thinking can only persist when based on personal experience. New thinking and behaviour is grounded in the positive "Aha!"

[2] David Rock and Jeffrey Schwartz "The Neuroscience of Leadership." *The Journal of Strength-based Interventions*, No. 3, USA, 2007.

experience of a new discovery or a new way of being in the world.

You need to focus to stay open to new impressions. When you let go of old patterns, there is a creative void before the new finds its form. By staying focused in the creative void, and being aware of all signs pointing in the same direction, you can let the new emerge.

You also need repeated encouraging attention from others to stay focused for long enough to let the new establish itself inside you, as well founded maps of reality. To experience that you are not alone in your reality, you need to share your map with others and discover that they have had similar experiences to yours.

So the brain´s economising with valuable energy keeps us on our well worn paths. To change your habits, you have to rewire your brain.

Summary of resistance to change

To change track, you have to rewire the brain. As the time for change comes closer, the polarisation is increasing between those in favour of change and those who don´t want to change their "winning concept". Our linear thinking in goal-means is well-established since school and is very efficient in managing everything that can be treated as a machine. Our maps of reality are often constructed on the same principles, built on clearly defined goals and problems. The more complex reality is, the more we become dependent on maps that give us a general view of the situation, and the more stuck we get in the language, symbols and measurements of the map.

Democratisation, globalisation and the need to formulate new goals and measures of progress makes the world of today much more like a living organism than a machine. To find new values, we have to look inside ourselves. But in our culture we are quite unprepared to deal with our inner world and share it with other people. Our habitual maps give us no guidance. We must create new maps of reality to guide us into sustainable development.

In school and in daily life we are trained to deal more with the symbolic world of maps than with reality itself, but before language made it possible to take over ready-made maps, as infants we participated in creating our own meaning-making maps by our interplay with our closest surroundings. Hopefully some of these skills can be reawakened and practiced in our construction of the new maps of today´s reality.

Development by interplay with the surroundings

We live, grow and find our place in the world by an ongoing interplay between needs and opportunities. Needs are signalled by our bodies while opportunities to satisfy them are found in our surroundings. By this interplay we create a meaningful order in the swarm of impressions from both inside and outside that bombard us from birth. That is how we create our first maps of reality, our world picture and our self image. By the direct interplay with the mother/care-giver we develop our sense of what is welcome/unwelcome, possible/impossible, safe/risky, what we have to do to get the attention we need, and so forth. Here the first patterns of our maps of reality are imprinted in our brain. As long as everything stays the same, these impressions remain as a valid map and we can develop routines for most of our responses.

Infants seek contact immediately after birth. They express strong signs of surprise and indignation when they don´t get expected responses on their attempts at making contact. They are totally dependent on the world of adults around them and count on being seen and met by them in their needs. Long before we have words for it, we get an experience of whether we can influence the world or not - whether it is benevolent, indifferent or hostile and whether I and my needs are worth respecting. So the first maps of reality are affective rather than cognitive and are beyond words. Only some kind of actual experience and emotional reaction can influence them.

This is why "moments of meeting" are so important in children´s development. As long as the interaction between infant and mother is "normal", the habitual maps remain unchanged. But now and then little surprises occur. Misunderstandings put them apart. It hurts when the infant pulls their mother's hair. Wills are colliding. This creates hot moments of personal disharmony that require reparation. The experience of being part of successful reparations of that kind gives the infant a feeling of self-esteem and a sense that it is possible to have a mutual interaction with the world. If they succeed in finding a new harmonious way of being together that neither of them has experienced before, they have taken a developmental step forward. Both have found a new attractive way of being in the world, unknown to them before. This is what Daniel Stern and other infant researchers call "moments of meeting", the healing power of the real "I-Thou-meeting"[3] that is so important in children´s maturation and in psychotherapy. But if the mother as a rule remains unreachable for contact, the infant will give up and become apathetic in its relationship with the world in the future.

As long as the interplay takes place on a preverbal level, the right brain hemisphere is the most active - that is the part of the brain responsible for the emotional assimilation of impressions, most often on a subconscious level. So our most profound self image is subconscious and unreachable by the intellect. These maps can only be influenced by real experiences of new possibilities that you didn´t know existed.

---

[3] In contrast to "I-It", subject-object, where the other is used as means to the subject´s goals.

At the age of three to four, the left brain hemisphere takes the lead. The speciality of the left half of the brain is linear, sequential and logical thinking - in contrast to that of the right hemisphere which works intuitively, non-linearly and holistically. With the emergence of language, readymade maps can be transmitted and swallowed without digestion. Maps that portray the experiences of others, or even ideas of how things should or could be according to wishful thinking. Maps that can only include aspects of life that are covered by words - often excluding the more formless and dynamic spiritual aspects of life. When these maps are handed over by authorities they are easily put as a filter between you and the real world, making you doubtful of your own direct experiences. If we want to create new maps that are better suited to guide us towards a sustainable development than the ones we are using today, it is important for us to recapture the skills to whole heartedly, and without filters of prejudice, interact with our environment as we did as infants.

Co-created development

As long as life goes on along its usual paths, it can be handled routinely, without awareness by the spinal cord. The routines assure you that everything is as usual. No change is demanded - at least not until you find your life too dull and unexciting. But suddenly something happens. Something that breaks the usual pattern and challenges the apprehension you have taken for granted. You wake up and feel alert. You become aware of the situation. If it is an unimportant incident, it may just pass as a little interruption of routine. But if it has an effect on your life, it will catch your interest. The unexpected event has to be met one way or the other. You have to do something about it.

At first, you look for solutions that you have tried before in similar situations, but if none of these resolve the situation, your tension will rise. You will have to devote increasing attention to the present situation and when you don´t find a solution you become more and more confused. Panic might arise when you realise that you don´t know what to do. You find yourself in a creative void, where you have to experiment to find an entirely new mode of interplay with the environment. This is where change and development starts. You notice that you have to act in a new and more aware way. You look inside yourself - into your emotional reactions, your interpretation of the situation, your impulses to action - for clues. By the responses from your environment to your more or less awkward efforts on managing the situation, you step by step gain ideas of where you can look for solutions.

By listening to your inner reactions, you get to know how you perceive the new situation that was the result of your actions and how you are affected by it. The response from outside will tell you how the surroundings perceive and react to your way of experiencing the situation and your attempts to act on it. As far as the parties that are involved in the situation are willing to share and try to understand each other's perspectives, the consciousness of the situation is widened to the sum of their perceptions of it. When the parties are able to make use of this shared richer reality, the chances of finding a common solution will improve - a solution where everybody can gain a profound and meaningful experience that shows that something more is possible than they are used to and habitually take for granted. Incidents that offer these kinds of deep insights stay in your mind as a moment of meeting.

Both personal development and organisational development can be fostered through this pattern. Although it is the same natural development process that we all have lived through as children, it requires some protection and special nourishment to be kept alive:

- Openness, honesty and trust are necessary ingredients in the process - a climate that is not granted in every company. It is a climate that must be created and nourished.
- In our project-oriented culture, built on thinking in terms of goal-means, we have great difficulties in letting go of control and staying in the creative void for long enough to let something new emerge. Instead of letting go of the old and well-known, we are tempted to jump to conclusions that are in line with our habitual apprehension, not giving the new enough time and space to evolve and show itself.
- Change is initiated by real experience of new possibilities. It is not enough to understand the situation as an interesting thought or idea. Your whole being must be engaged.
- You reach a truly shared reality by dialogue - not by arguing and trying to convince each other about rightness of your own opinions, which is so common in most discussions.

How can we share each other's perspectives?

Gestalt was originally developed as a therapy method. People look for therapy when they feel that something is wrong with their lives, but they don´t know what that is. This is rather like the present situation in the world - something is wrong, but what? - Gestalt has well-tried tools with which to meet these kinds of situations.

Gestalt is based on Martin Buber´s "I-Thou-contact" (dialogue) and mindfulness. That is the right, if not the duty, for every human being to have a personal relationship with whatever they are meeting in their lives - other people, the meaning of work, nature, the world, life itself.

It is very much about personal choice and responsibility. The choice to meet the world with open senses and an open heart, and take responsibility for your choices and non-choices in your private life as well as in your working and social lives. As Gestaltists, we are consciously trained for a much higher degree of inner guidance and self-support than is common in society today; to answer for who you are.

Gestalt is phenomenology in practice. This means that the world as it is perceived from different perspectives is in focus. Instead of trying to find a once and for all given objective truth, we acknowledge everybody´s perspective as a valid part of total reality. What feels relevant to pay attention to may change according to what needs are guiding the attention. So as Gestaltists we try to gather people from all involved perspectives to deal with their shared situation together. In different ways we try to support them in sharing their perspectives with each other; how they perceive the situation, how they are affected by it, what they have seen, thought, felt and how they have felt compelled to act.

We don´t just talk about the situation. Instead we employ a variety of techniques such as visualisation, guided fantasies, role-play, family constellations, making pictures, movement, dialogue and the empty chair to get a concrete experience of it in the present moment. A now where senses as well as feelings and thoughts are engaged, because we take in the whole experience as an internalised representation to guide us in similar situations in the future. It is the skill of dealing with tricky situations that we will train. "Give a hungry man a fish and he will satisfy his hunger for one day - or teach him to fish", a Chinese proverb says.

When you learn to cycle, it is not the bicycle in itself that you internalise, but the interplay between the bicycle, the rider and the terrain you are biking in. It is about movement, feeling, visual impressions and experiences of balance and speed. It is the whole experience you take in as an instructive representation that you can use in future cycle rides on other bikes, in other terrains.

It is very rare that you can obtain the complete picture from one point of view. The ability to see from different angles gives a widened consciousness. We have to listen to each other and be curious about others' points of view, instead of immediately asserting our own position as soon as somebody else is experiencing the situation in another way from his perspective. By gathering observations from all involved, we share a reality, which is available for everybody. When this is done, we can start to interpret the situation together to find out what we want to do about it. By intuitively grouping observations in different ways, we can see if any meaningful patterns emerge. What kind of messages do we find in the observations?

This is very much in line with phenomenological, qualitative research. When you start with a clear idea about the situation, and have a clearly formulated hypothesis that you want to prove, then you can employ a quantitative research approach. But when you want to find out more about the whole situation, you have to use a qualitative approach. And this is the case when we try to change our habits, because they are harmful to our planet, when we try to give our economy a more qualitative content instead of continuing to fill it with polluting material things. When we are looking for better ways to relate to each other, in ways that make better use of our differences and nourish our self-respect and open space for our own initiatives, making it possible and easier to live together in peace. In this transformation we have to make use of everybody´s perspective and we have to stimulate everybody´s wish to contribute. Here is an arena for co-creation of something new. A co-creation where everybody´s contribution is welcome, including those who are not used to being listened to and who have had experiences that nobody has cared about before. We must give them time, space and a structure in which to share their experiences in ways that are perceived as meaningful.

Liberation from the comparison game

Consumption above what is enough to satisfy our basic needs is socially conditioned. Aspiration for more is about competition in a comparison hierarchy, a competition for appreciation and a sense of belonging of the kind that is characterised by what Hans Zetterberg has labelled "outer-directed" people (see page 27). One way of putting an end to over consumption can be to liberate ourselves from the comparison game. We can find ways in which to satisfy inner values without taking a roundabout way via status symbols. We can learn to feel good enough to find contentment and the ability to enjoy what we meet and enjoy the sense of appreciation and belonging without needing external measures of being especially successful. This is where we can really profit from training mindfulness, which, according to Csikszentmihalyi, can nourish the sense of flow and happiness in life (see page 14).

The dominance of the ego

What forces are driving us into the comparison game? According to Eckhart Tolle it is the ego at work. What we say about people who are boastful and arrogant show-offs is that they have a "big ego". The ego is fed by comparisons and competition. It will never be satisfied. The ego mostly compares itself with those who are better off, seldom with those who are less successful. The important thing is the ambition - the aspiration to reach the standards of "competitors". But the need for "more" is a bottomless hole that is impossible to fill. When you have reached what you have aspired to, there are always others in a "higher division" to compete with. The ego has a very undeveloped ability to stop and enjoy what it already has. All the time it is looking for something more, bigger, more exclusive, faster, more up to date etc.

To be able to compare itself with others, the ego looks for evident and controllable measures. Inner values based on your own experiences are not good enough (for example, that I like this better than that). No, competition is going on in the public world and requires measures that are visible to everybody. This is where fashion plays an important role, where trend setters agree on what ideals will be right for the next period. Then the ego tries to be as perfect as possible according to these ideals. Your value as a human is measured by how well you succeed or fail in this aspiration.

The attention of the ego is totally directed towards how we are looked on by others. The ego has no contact with our inner world. The meaning of life is about how well you succeed in reaching prevailing goals and norms. Therefore, the ego is very urgent in denominating and explaining everything. Only phenomena that are describable, measurable and controllable are valid. It is also very important that the ideals will sustain and that people are loyal to them. Those who question agreed values and ideas threaten the whole safety of the ego, so public measures have to be defended at all prices. This is where fundamentalism and dogmatism has their basis. Your whole life will float away if you don´t have any inner grounds to anchor in.

The need of the ego to be at the centre of everyone's attention carries traits of paranoia. The suspicion that everybody would be occupied by pursuing just me is egocentric, whether it is triggered by arrogance or by compensation for the sense that nobody sees me and cares about me. It will feed a defensive attitude to the environment. The collective ego of tribes, clans, nations and religious groups also has traits of paranoia; it is we, the good ones, against the rest who are the evil ones.

There is nothing wrong with the ego as such. We all have our ego within us. We need some appreciation and feedback to feel proud of our successes. And we can feel awkward in certain situations. Of course it can be wise of you to keep informed about on what grounds you will probably be judged in society, or in certain groupings or cultures, and what expectations people have of you and what responses will hurt or offend them. The ego helps us in our orientation in society and to make well calculated choices. But we are not only ego. We need to be aware that the ego is stimulated and start leading our behaviour in order to be able to free ourselves from its dominant grip; because in the world of today, the ego seems to have a too dominant place.

Survival strategies

Life and survival is a co-creation between the organism and its environment. It is about the ability to adapt to different living conditions and to find and assimilate the opportunities for life that are offered by the surroundings and to protect oneself from and avoid threats. An acorn contains the potential for becoming a perfect oak tree. If it is planted in an open field with good living conditions, it will grow into a big and harmonious oak. If it takes root in a narrow crevice of a mountain, it will take another form. The roots will have to stretch out in different directions in search for water and nourishment. And it will grow in forms where the mountain leaves living space for it. It will be perfect for this situation, and quite interesting and beautiful.

While a plant cannot move away from where its seed has taken root, and only has a passive defence mechanism, an animal can also try fight and flight strategies or consciously move away to a place with better living conditions. As we humans came late in the evolution chain, we contain all the former species that we developed from. And we have surpassed instinctual survival strategies and added meaning and value to our lives by our ability to reflect on life. But if you look at a foetus from a pig and a human at an early stage of development, it is almost impossible to discriminate between the two. And we have to survive before we can give meaning to our life. This is another aspect of economising with precious brainpower.

All the survival strategies that we learnt as infants and children can prevent us from seeing the world as it is now when we are grown up and more independent than we were. Amygdala in the limbic system prevents us from putting our fingers into boiling water twice. The next time we try, our whole body shouts, "Don´t do it! It hurts!" This is very good. The bad thing is that these defence reflexes are so "stupid". They are governed subconsciously by the old reptile brain and are unreachable by the intellect. Amygdala cannot differentiate between now and then, or between a real and an imagined tiger. It reacts with the same fear as if the painful experience that originated the warning signal is going to be repeated. And this is not very wise, because much of what was experienced as "boiling water" by a defenceless and dependent little child can be harmless for an adult with much greater capacity to say "no" or go somewhere else. And the frightening experience may create irrelevant cause-effect-connections. If, for example, a lady in a red coat happened to pass as I had a shocking car accident, the sight of a red coat may trigger the same fear as the accident did. As these defence reflexes are buried deep down in the unconscious and emotional layers of the brain; you cannot reach them by words to try to change them. They are only susceptible to real experience. So you have to put your fingers into what your whole body thinks is "boiling water" to find out that it does not hurt any more. Not until then will the automatic defence reflexes loosen their grip. This is how we, by Gestalt therapy, try to complete unfinished business by creating situations where the client can experience that something else is possible other than what his earlier painful experiences have taught him to believe.

Painful experiences that are not worked through, finished and left to history, stay in the body and colour our view of the world. We can dwell on the same injury over and over again, stocking up our anger, urge for revenge, defensiveness and longing for rehabilitation. On a collective plane, this can result in fights between groups and in terrorism. As long as we are looking for an external explanation of our inner state of mood, unfinished business will stay in the body, nourishing negative thoughts. Conflict, or the idea that the world is hostile or unjust, can explain our bad feelings. If we are unaware of the pain we carry inside, we often project it onto the environment, believing that we feel bad because of a hostile world, and we develop a defensive attitude. If we act as if they have a secret motive when we meet people who really are benevolent, they don´t feel seen and can feel insulted. If this happens, in the end they feel hostile and we get what we expected from our prejudiced suspicion. We get the response that we unconsciously ask for.

Even when accusations may be justifiable, you stay trapped in your ego as long as you blame others for your feelings. And you see yourself as a victim rather than as an adult responsible for your own life. So there is only one guilty perpetrator: human unawareness.

Let go of unrealistic wishful thinking

The main reason for staying unhappy is seldom the situation as such, but your thoughts about it. Often your thoughts about how it should be or could be according to ideals and ideas of different kinds hurt much more than reality itself. That is the wisdom behind Alcoholics Anonymous's prayer:

God, grant me the serenity to accept the things I cannot change,
Courage to change the things I can,
And wisdom to know the difference.

The world is not always how we wish it to be. It is what it is. Accepting this is not a passive and powerless submission, rather it is a decision to put awareness and energy where you can make use of it. A decision to pay attention to what really exists, rather than to what is only fantasy, thoughts, fears, dreams, unfinished business etc; all that doesn´t exist but is missing according to ideas and norms.

These were the conclusions that Byron Katie[4] came to when she one day in 1986 woke up from a deep depression at a treatment home. Suddenly all her black

---

4 Byron Katie (2002): *"Loving What Is"*

thoughts were gone and happiness could find its way into her heart. From that day on, her sense of life has grown stronger and stronger inside her.

When she tried to understand what had changed her life, she saw the pattern and developed the liberating steps of "The Work[5]". She formulated a battery of questions that could help us to become aware of how useless, and even destructive, it is to become stuck in sources of irritation that we all too often are unable to do anything about.

1. Think of the person or situation that you think is poisoning your life! List everything you think is wrong and should be different! Be honest and express your real feelings and thoughts. This is a way to become aware and get your anger out of your body. These are facts. This is how you think and feel. It is time to own your perception, conclusions and the fact that you are the one who is irritated. Your description is not an absolute and objective truth of the situation.

2. Ask yourself if your life would really become so much better if the situation or person would change the way that you wish! What would be better? How? Try to answer this with an open heart - and be specific! How would you experience it?

3. What is hurting you the most? Is it the situation as such, or is it your images of how it should be? Is it reality, or your picture of reality? Look at each of your statements! How are they affecting you, what feelings are evoked? Are they helping you to meet the world in a satisfying way? What would it be like for you, if the thought disappeared, if you could let go of it?

---

[5] www.thework.com

Very often what is especially irritating are traits we dislike in ourselves. Here the other person openly expresses traits of life that I fear and would be too ashamed of showing myself!

4. Try to give judgement about the situation or other person to yourself! Say: "I should ..!" etc. What happens to you when you do that? Does it ring any bells?

This is a personal job, something you do for yourself. It is not for the ears of the other. It is about accepting responsibility for your own reactions, which can help you in your contact with the environment later on. To recognise facts is always strengthening. Reality will always win in the long run, whether we like it or not. What you think causes a lot of what you feel. So instead of being your thoughts and feelings be the awareness behind them!

Ego driven work

When your work is driven by the ego, you work in order to get recognition, profit or power. Then work is used for something else than it is intended for. It becomes a kind of "instead-of...", a detour towards the desired goal. The ego is not able to stay in the now to meet what is. Instead striving is its ongoing drive. Therefore, the ego has three dysfunctional ways of dealing with the present moment according to Eckhart Tolle (2005):

- as a means to a future end,
- as an obstacle or
- as an enemy.

Means to an end: The future only exists as a thought. You are never wholeheartedly present as long as you are occupied by getting somewhere else - to the goal which you dream of attaining and which is of another kind than what you are doing right now. Mountaineers in Himalaya from the West noticed that although they were very tired when they pitched camp, their Sherpas seldom were. When they tried to find out why, they discovered that their Sherpas were always present in the now. They were where they were, on their way, and could enjoy the wandering in itself, the sun shining on them, the beautiful views, the flowers beside the path, the butterfly they met. But the Westerners were aiming at the top of the mountain and got caught by how far it still was to get there. Instead of focusing on their present reality, they were occupied by what they did not have, by what was missing between the now and the goal. They could not rest in the now and enjoy it.

An obstacle to overcome: Life is looked on as a long row of problems that have to be solved before you can be happy and feel good enough to start living. Happiness is conditional and has to be earned. You cannot just accept it and receive it as it is offered in the present moment. This is where impatience, frustration and stress have their origin.

Enemy: When you go on doing things that you dislike, when you scold and cannot get over things that have happened to you and see the world in terms of "should" and "should not", of guilt and blame, then you are judging what is already fact. Then the external reality mirroring your internal state of mind is perceived as hostile. When you treat the world as hostile, it often lives up to your expectations and becomes hostile.

From "I-It" to "I-Thou"

The ego has an instrumental view on the environment and sees it as a means to something or a cause of its own inner condition. The ego has an "I-It-relation" - a subject-object-relation - to its surroundings. The environment is there to be dealt with in one way or another. The ego always has to do something in order to ...

The ego also takes an active part in the comparison game, which has to do with "doing". It is about how well you are doing in relation to others, if you are good enough to earn the appreciation of others and also if you are too competent, evoking jealousy in others. Instead of being able to enjoy somebody who is extraordinary capable, pleasant, ambitious, beautiful or brave, there is often a lot of bullshit and gossip spread in the corridors and at the coffee-tables, where s/he is seen as an "unfair" measure of what you should be like.

One way of liberating yourself from the comparison game is by breaking the dominance of the ego. While the ego´s relationships to its surroundings are very much on an I-It-basis, you can try the alternative: "I-Thou" - a subject-subject-relationship. The concept "I-Thou" was introduced by the philosopher Martin Buber, who further elaborated the personal existential meeting with the environment that the existentialists were focusing on. I-Thou is the genuine and wholehearted personal meeting with another person or a phenomenon in the world. Inclusion and empathy is a vital part of the I-Thou-meeting, where you try to experience the situation from the other´s point of view, to let yourself be touched by the other without losing your own sense of self. It is the meeting between two (or more) subjects who mutually recognise each other´s right to exist according to their own conditions.

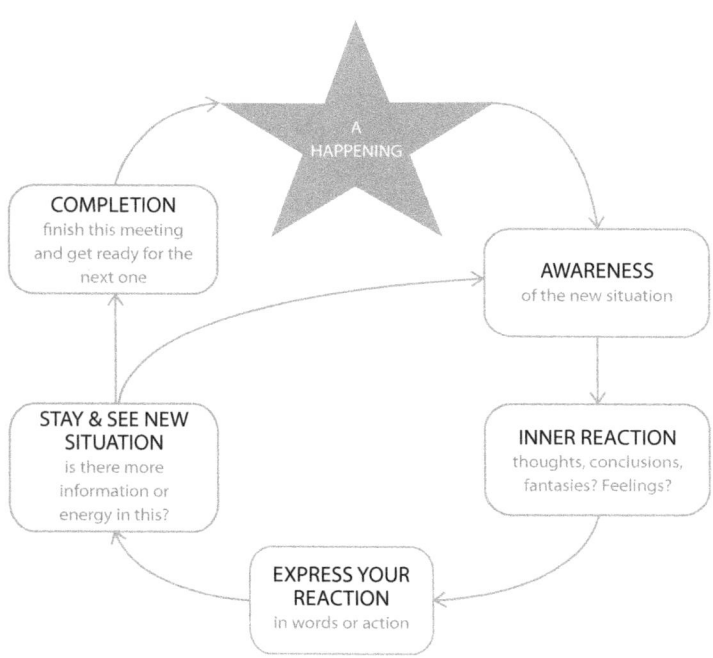

Figure 1 "I-Thou-meeting" or "Contact" according to Gestalt

The I-Thou-meeting does not just occur between people, but is an attitude towards the world. You can meet a bird, a tree, a sound, the sunshine, the rain or whatever with the whole of your being, body and soul. It is the act of being affected by it in one way or another (becoming surprised, happy, impressed, captured, curious, sad, angry, scared or calm) and in words or action giving some kind of response (enjoying it, running away, attacking, touching it, caressing it, examining it, tasting it, giving a verbal response). It means staying and interacting with it until the meeting is experienced as complete, because it has no more information to offer and the energy is fading from it. When you are finished with it and have lost interest in it, you are ready to meet the next situation. This is how we learn more and more about the world and about ourselves in the world - this is how we design our maps of reality.

The search for an I-Thou-meeting can also be initiated by internal signals such as thirst, hunger, boredom, lust, loneliness etc. Then we look for a solution in our surroundings and we have all the inner reactions that can be evoked in the meeting process described in Figure 1. These are the thoughts, conclusions, fantasies, hopes, fears and longings that can be evoked by the actual situation - and which probably are coloured by more or less subconscious needs and frustrated needs from before.

While the I-It-attitude of the ego is very focused on doing, the I-Thou-attitude gives much more space for just being. Being and enjoying what you are meeting. Being curious and open to what is happening in the situation, without being occupied by and focused on a specific end result.

Here and now

The I-Thou-meeting can only take place here and now. Like the I-Thou-meeting, "here and now" is about the concrete phenomenological experience, in contrast to the more intellectual "talk about" there and then as an interesting story out there that you don´t need to relate to personally and emotionally. A story where you exchange opinions, rather than first hand experiences. So here and now is about something more than just the time-dimension. It is about the quality of the meeting. Here and now I can be very aware of and moved by something that happened there and then. The memory can be so alive in me that I can meet it as if it were happening here and now. Therefore we also call it conscious presence or mindfulness. It is where I meet "what is" with my whole being, whether it is an actual person or situation or a memory, dream, thought or something else which is vivid in my consciousness here and now and which is quite different from intellectual discussions about what should or could be according to ideals and ideas of different kinds.

This personal meeting with what is, is the core of phenomenology. We don´t live in an absolute, objective and measurable world, but in the subjectively experienced world. As a Gestalt therapist I feel at home with the core-concepts of phenomenology: "the lived world", "the lived body" and "inter-subjectivity". And this is not very odd, because we are children of the same spirit. Apart from Eastern philosophy, Gestalt is founded on existentialism, phenomenology and Gestalt psychology. Merleau-Ponty, one of the founders of modern phenomenology was a good friend of Sartre (existentialist) before he met Husserl (the founder of phenomenology). And Gestalt psychology and phenomenology had a strong influence on each other. Both Merleau-Ponty and Fritz Perls (the founder of Gestalt therapy) worked with Goldstein treating brain-damaged soldiers from the First World War and learned a lot about the interconnection of body and mind (what is called neuro-psychology today).

One of the most important tools in Gestalt therapy is that of phenomenological focusing - staying with what is here and now. It involves becoming curious and aware of all phenomena that are activated in the actual I-Thou-meeting and how they interact with each other.

- What am I catching with my senses - seeing, hearing, smelling, tasting and sensing (outer zone)?
- What is happening in my body? What feelings, body-sensations, survival-reflexes, tensions, butterflies in

my stomach, palpitations, tears, warmth, ache and impulses to act am I aware of (inner zone)?
- What thoughts do I notice? What interpretations, conclusions, fantasies, hopes, fears, memories and judgements am I aware of (intermediate zone)?

Notice what is happening in all three contact zones and scrutinise their interplay with each other to find out what we can learn from that! This is important for a real and genuine contact, an I-Thou-meeting. This kind of interplay between environment, body and mind is also what characterises mindfulness or conscious presence.

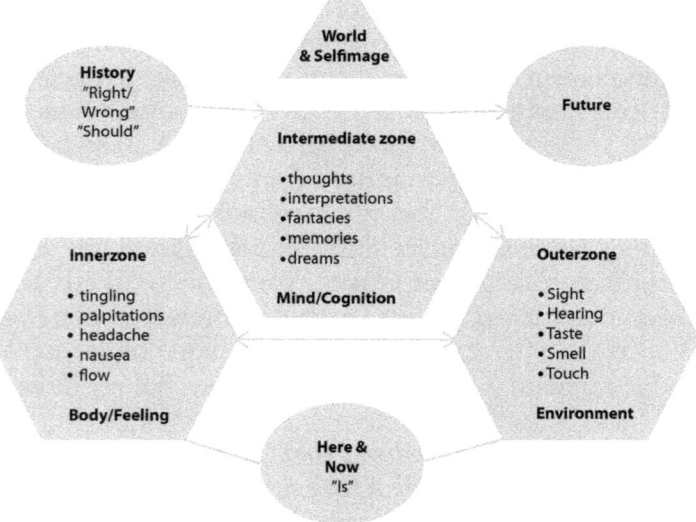

Figure 2 The interplay between the environment, body and soul

Already recognising what is and becoming aware of it will probably promote a change (the paradoxical theory of change). You can only move from the place you are standing. Stay there for a while, look around with awareness and notice your reactions; you will find out if you want to move and, if so, in what direction. If I as a therapist or consultant changes from I-Thou to I-It and starts having ambitions for you, you will probably get defensive and we will find ourselves in a struggle. "Don´t push the river!" Perls says. The aim of Gestalt is to encourage people´s own choices and own responsibility. As Gestalt therapists or consultants we can try to point to what is, and by experiments offer experiences of new possibilities and choice situations - insofar as you are willing to participate.

So to support somebody is not primarily about doing something with the other. Just being with her and supporting her in experiencing what she is experiencing at this very moment allows her to get a glimpse of what is possible - a glimpse of what is already there inside her. This is what is called "satori" in the zen tradition - a moment of presence when you switch off the voice in your head with all its thoughts and the feelings it evokes.

The best you can offer - is yourself

When you are present, when your attention is wholeheartedly in the now, this will be observable in what you are doing. For example, pay attention to how you are affected by being close to people who are occupied by what they are doing - a musician who is one with his music, a child who is totally present in her play, an intensive and close dialogue. You are present when what you are doing is satisfying in itself and not only a means to an end (money, prestige, to win). You are present when you feel joy and vitality in what you are doing.

Critique and blame is an attack against the ego, which immediately tries to restore itself by self-righteousness, defence or counter-attack. Instead of defending yourself, try to do nothing. When you stop justifying yourself, and are not trying to strengthen your self-image, you let go of your identification with the external form and give your being, your essence, a chance to emerge. If you feel good enough without being somebody special, if you feel OK without having to be perfect or excellent, if you are satisfied and comfortable in being who you are, then you are in harmony with the force of the universe.

I myself struggled a lot with the theme of not being good enough. Maybe that was the reason why I encouragingly wrote, "The best you can offer - is yourself!" in invitations to seminars of different kinds. And I meant it. You can never be better than being present with the whole of your being in each moment, wholeheartedly offering what you want to offer, without keeping a part of you occupied with judging yourself by comparisons and self-blame. I wanted to give participants in my groups a real experience of this, and when this thought left my head and fell down into my stomach as a fact, not only valid for others, but also for me, then my whole life turned around. Then I let go of my identification with my ego.

Being wholeheartedly present in what you are actually doing is something that people understand in the world of sports. This is what makes the tennis player concentrate on each ball in itself without thinking of the score of the match. The pressing expectations on the favourites can make them lose against clearly inferior competitors. If you think of the gold medal instead of surrendering to the running, you will never win. Sports stars know what presence is through their own experience and by mental training.

The universe of forms and beyond forms

The reason why people from such a result-oriented world as the sports world understand fuzzy concepts as those above is probably because of the quick payoff in better results. But for many others in our result-oriented culture it seems incredible that good results will come when we stop thinking about them, when we let go of end-games. I am back to the difficulty of explaining what the new approach is. Until now I have described it in terms of what it is not: It is not goal-means-thinking. It is not MORE of what we are already having or doing. It is not identifying with the ego or the role of the victim. But what *is* the new approach? The keyword is conscious presence, mindfulness, but presence in what?

Tolle attempts to explain this by separating awareness about objects from consciousness about space. The lives of most people are filled with things: material things, things to do and things to think of. This consciousness of objects needs to be balanced by consciousness of space, which means that apart from being aware of things (including sensory impressions, feelings and thoughts) you are also aware of the undercurrent of consciousness where you are aware of being conscious and where you can reflect on your own being.

If you have had an experience of wonder when you have been looking up into the sky, or even a sense of reverence of its inexplicable mysteries, then for a moment you have let go of your eagerness to dominate and explain and have become aware of not only the things in the sky, but also of the eternal depth of the universe. When your eye finds nothing to watch, this nothingness is experienced as open space. When your ear finds nothing to hear, you experience stillness. Our senses are designed to perceive the universe of forms and, when they encounter an absence of form, the formless consciousness which underlies the perception can emerge into the open and make all kinds of experience possible.

When you hear about inner space, maybe you start looking for it as if you are looking for a thing or an experience, but you will never find it that way because it resides inside you. For example, there is a common characteristic feature of the ability to experience beauty, to appreciate simple things, to enjoy one's own company and to meet others with a loving kindness. It is about the contentedness, peace and vitality, which are there invisibly in the background and without which the experience would be impossible. We have a couple of inherent capabilities that are part of life itself - the ability to recognise what is more life than something else when we are meeting it.

It is from the inner space, from the unconditioned consciousness itself, that true happiness and joy of life has its origin. To be aware of little, insignificant events your inner energies must be free and open, where you can have an alert and unprejudiced awareness. So, take some deep breaths to come home to yourself! Be quiet! Listen! Be present! Experience the meaning of I AM, here, in this world, right now!

The left and right brain hemispheres

Jill Bolte Taylor[6], a neurologist, had a startling experience of the formless world when her left brain hemisphere was wiped out by a stroke. When the blood vessel broke, she gradually lost her capability to walk, talk, read, write and remember anything from her life. She also lost her sense of boundaries between herself and the environment and experienced herself as an inseparable one with

---

6 See her lecture at www.ted.com.

everything else. She lost her ability to communicate, but she felt very alive. And as Jill Bolte Taylor was a scientist, she was curious about what was happening and could study it from within.

By losing the cells responsible for linear and sequential thinking, she had to let her right brain hemisphere take over her experiencing. This gave her another view on consciousness than her training as a neurologist had given her, and she became very aware of consciousness as a threefold process - cognitive, emotional and physical - and how the body responds to thoughts and emotions.

When she could only use the consciousness of her right brain hemisphere, she also gained quite another experience of the world, herself and life than she was used to - and trained for. With no boundaries, You and I were totally confluent in a We as members of the human family. In the beginning, she felt as if she were in a state of nirvana, where the world was filled with compassionate loving people and all senses were present in the now, attending what was happening here and now. She had a feeling of euphoria which is not happiness, but a sense of contentedness - neither positive nor negative, but rather a kind of content acceptance.

Christer Perfjell had a very similar experience. He was an insurance broker with no previous experience of the spiritual or psychological world. He broke his neck in an accident with a freestyle jump on skies. His whole body said, *No, don't do it!* just before this particular jump, but his friend encouraged him and he jumped, resulting in this sad outcome.

After four years of painful recovery from the physical damage, avoiding paralysis and the like, he started to have startling experiences. His intuition and gut-feeling was tremendously enhanced. He had out of the body experiences that he had never had before. He had a feeling of what was going to happen, before events actually occurred. Now and then he suddenly found himself in another world, experienced as at least as real as the present world. A world which was very peaceful and full of compassionate people who were caring about each other. It was very similar to Jill Bolte Taylor´s paradise and with many of the qualities of the formless world that Eckhart Tolle describes.

At first, Christer Perfjell found these experiences very frightening, and in his fear of being looked upon as crazy he didn´t share them with anybody else. But as he got more and more used to them, his curiosity drove him to look for some kind of understanding. The answers he first found were too wishy-washy for him. He wanted more scientific explanations to be satisfied. So he turned to the Center for Conscious Studies (CCS) in Tucson, Arizona[7] and has followed their annual conferences since then.

In one experiment they measured his EEG and were alarmed by its high frequency, fearing that he was going to have an epileptic attack. He had the same EEG as a Tibetan monk who had been meditating for his whole life, so something had happened physiologically after the accident.

As all these experiences of the formless world emanating from the right brain hemisphere are quite similar to what is described as spiritual experiences in spiritual literature, they invite speculation. Could it be that the more holistic right hemisphere of the brain is designed

---

[7] Se www.consciousness.arizona.edu.

to deal with the formless spiritual world, while the left hemisphere is designed to deal with the world of forms here on Earth? And could it be that the left hemisphere has been so favoured in our society that it has taken almost total control of our ways of experiencing the world and ourselves in the world?

Anyway, whatever we call it, holistic thinking is vital to our sense of being alive and experiencing meaning in our lives. And still, at school and in our culture at large, the left hemisphere is overemphasised compared to the right brain hemisphere. Science activates our left hemisphere where logic and linear thinking reside and what we cannot prove is often regarded as fiction, not real. Measurability is important. But at least as important is the context, the totality, how everything is related to each other and the mysteries of life. And the ability to deal with these holistic issues is another kind of skill that requires its own training, but at school, music, art and physical movement, which activate the right hemisphere, are often downgraded.

Different dimensions of reality

In their book *Sensitelligent - A guide to Life* (2010) Ralph Jenkins and Marie Örnesved also discriminated between the intuitive holistic thinking of the right brain hemisphere dealing with wholes and overall patterns from the logical, sequential, linear thinking of the left hemisphere. Where the left hemisphere is focused on survival, the right hemisphere is more focused on living a rich, meaningful and joyous life. This is their dividing line between logic and intuition. Jenkins and Örnesved discuss the four or more dimensional world, 4D (the quantum world) being our intuition and about being, contemplation and more spiritual consciousness based on universal laws. Logic, according to them, is the three dimensional world, 3D (the Newton-world, the world of our senses), and is based on doing, reasoning, control and measurability. 3D is an evolution from the survival instincts of lower dimensions and is helping us to find means for satisfying our basic material needs and to develop rules and norms which help us to live together in peace and harmony.

While 3D is focused on doing and how to deal with our duties here on earth, 4D is about our being, how we enrich our lives and give them meaning, how we can live in trust and love and dare to trust the power of love, even if our previous experiences show something else, how we accept what is and surrender to life - trusting the process.

Trust and intuition: the attitudes of 4D
In their book Jenkins and Örnesved identify a number of attitudes leading to and based on trust and intuition. Those of you who want to go deeper into the concepts and their relationship to each other can get excellent guidance from their book[8]. Here I only mention them and leave the rest to the reader´s own ability to meditate over them and take care of the learnings they can bring. So concentrate on each one of the attitudes listed below, one by one! Close your eyes, take some deep breaths, repeat the attitude silently to yourself and notice what thoughts, feelings and reflections they trigger!

---

[8] Jenkins R and Örnesved M (2010) *Sensitelligent*. Matador, Troubador Publishing.

I ACCEPT
I AM IN MY POWER
I AM PRESENT
I AM UNDERSTANDING MY PAIN
I ASK FOR ADVICE AND GUIDANCE
I CREATE THROUGH INTUITION
I DECIDE
I FOLLOW MY INNER COMPASS
I FORGIVE
I LOVE MYSELF FOR WHO I AM
I LOVE OTHERS FOR WHO THEY ARE
I SAY NO TO OLD THOUGHT PATTERNS
I SPEAK MY TRUTH WITH CLARITY
I STAY OPEN TO RECEIVE THE UNEXPECTED
I TAKE RESPONSIBILITY FOR MY ACTIONS
I TAKE RESPONSIBILITY FOR MY FEELINGS
I TRUST
MY PRESENCE IS NEUTRAL

You can find a picture of this at www.sensitelligent.com - where you can also find a representation of the clouds of 3D which can confuse the experience of 4D.

Fear and control
What can sabotage our efforts to live in 4D are some attitudes of 3D which are triggered by a lack of trust:

ANGER
DENIAL
DOUBT
ESCAPE
EXPECTATIONS

FEAR
GUILT
IDENTITY
PAIN
PAST EXPERIENCE
PROJECTION
PROTECTION
REJECTION
SPECULATION
STRESS
THE EGO
WORRY

Again we see the wrestling between guidance from within and guidance from others, between the holistic views of 4D anchored in universal laws and 3D´s flux between quickly changing and short sighted demands and expectations from other people, and the emotional storms triggered by this struggle. But it is not about either-or, but rather both-and. Both dimensions are valid at the same time.

When I was a teenager, I often brought my troubles with me out into the forest to share them with a leaf, instead of worrying my parents with them. Seventeen years old and unhappily in love, I could from the bottom of my heart share that life was not worth living. As the leaf I could answer myself, OK my lad, it is true that this hurts a lot. At the same time, you are seventeen years old and life is much longer. Out there are many wonderful girls you have not yet met. So the chances are good that love will blossom again and you will find life worth living once more. For me, it was very healing both to share the pain and to look at the situation from a wider and less entangled perspective. Although they contradicted each other, both perspectives were equally true.

In comparison with the earthly concrete three dimensional world, the more spiritual 4D world can be experienced as very abstract and esoteric, as a fantasy or as wishful thinking rather than reality. But that so many people have had similar spiritual experiences, among them Jill Bolte Taylor and Christer Perfjell, and can feel some meaning in many spiritual concepts indicates that they are reality one way or another. Apart from residing in the right brain hemisphere, which is difficult to reach by words (other than metaphors), their esoteric nature may have to do with the lack of available observational instruments.

Even though Newton´s physics is good enough for explaining most observable phenomena, Einstein´s physics opened up entirely new dimensions. Einstein and the quantum physicists discovered that the world could be understood as either matter or energy ($e=mc^2$). They were studying the microcosmos, beyond cellular, molecular and atomic levels, down to a subatomic and quantum level where the difference between the atomic and subatomic world is as huge as the difference between the world of stones and trees that we perceive with our senses and the atomic level. On these levels, scientists found that what we call matter is in reality 99.9% empty space. That far is the distance between the atoms compared to their size and there is the same amount of space within each atom. And furthermore, everything is related to everything else with a consistent exchange of energy. That is what reality looks like according to quantum physicists.

As a matter of fact, we live in the Newtonian world and the quantum world at the same time. As long as objects have a mass big enough to cause a magnetic field, they comply with Newton´s laws. Objects with a smaller mass follow the laws of quantum physics. And the smaller objects are incorporated in the larger ones.

The quantum world can behave strangely. For example, light can present itself as particles (photons) or as waves. If a researcher wants to study light in its form of particles, that is how the light will present itself. So at the quantum level there are no objective observers, as the intention of the observer will affect the outcome. Science does not know how this happens, but its occurrence is an agreed on fact. The phenomenon is called "Bell´s Theorem". An interesting fact is that the synapses, the gaps between the nerve cells in our brain, are of the same size as objects on the border between the Newtonian world and the quantum world. The two worlds seem to meet in our brain. This might explain something of how thoughts can affect the body - where thoughts from the quantum world interact with physiological phenomena in the Newtonian world (and a lot of parapsychological phenomena as well).

Energy will go where you focus your awareness. For example, be aware of your left hand for a while and notice what is happening. Then shift your awareness to your stomach and notice what is happening. My guess is that after a while you will feel some kind of flow where you put your awareness. Or some pain or tension if your energy is blocked there. Apart from being a material organism governed by chemical reactions of different kinds, humans can also be seen as energy beings. We can talk about life energy or life flow as something formless.

The trouble is that words belong to the world of forms in the left brain hemisphere and cannot transmit formless experiences. They must be experienced directly, one way or another, by the right brain hemisphere. Can I sense my inner space, my own presence, the experience of "I am"? Am I aware of not only what is happening right now, but also of the now itself as the living timeless inner space in which everything happens? Try by sharpening your attention to nothing! This is the ability that most forms of meditation are designed to practice by a stillness that can block the usual chatter of thoughts.

To liberate yourself from imprisonment in habitual thought patterns, maps of reality or other kinds of forms, you have to accept impressions from the environment or from within just as they are, without trying to understand them, interpret them or categorise them into some well known structure. You need to open your senses and stay with a sound, scrutinise it, work out how it fits into other sounds, whether you like it or not, etc. before jumping into conclusions that it is a car coming from town to visit your neighbour. Or you need to stay for a while with the signals from your body, without trying to control them or interpret them. Let them live their own life - and be aware of what is happening. Let them progress in their own way and at their own pace, guiding you for a tour inside your body revealing what kind of life is expressed there, maybe giving you a surprising message. This is what we call "phenomenological focusing" or the "awareness continuum" in Gestalt. It is very much about staying in the creative void long enough to let something new emerge. The void where we let go of our habitual goal-means-thinking and surrender to what is. Where we let our being fill our doing, not to get lost in our doing and get trapped in any prescribed "in order to".

Live who you are!

You are here on Earth to live your life as the person you are by interacting with the world you live in. Nobody from outside has the right to define who you are or how you want to live your life. Only you can do that by the interplay between your needs and desires on one hand, and the opportunities to satisfy these offered by the environment on the other, or the demands and expectations on you by the environment and your response to these.

The ego has a tendency to create antagonism in society by fragmenting reality into yours or mine, right or wrong, winners or losers. Actions that do not trigger counteractions are those aiming at creating something good for everyone involved. They are not in the service of my country, but of mankind, not to further my religion but to support the consciousness of all people, not in favour of my species but good for nature and all living beings. The more you can liberate yourself from your egocentricity, your unrealistic desires to control life and the usual fragmentation of reality into either-or, the richer your exchange of the interaction with the environment will be.

When you let go of your desire to explain and designate, you can experience the undercurrent of conscious presence, mindfulness. When you experience that what you are doing is in harmony with who are, you are experiencing mindfulness. It is not what you are doing, but how you are doing it that defines to what extent you are expressing your inner aim to become conscious and stay conscious in your real life.

The joy of co-creation

There are three phenomena that help you to notice when your work and what else you are doing is in harmony with who you are and "what is", that is how conscious your activity is: acceptance, joy and enthusiasm.

Acceptance: Right now this situation and this moment demands of me that I do this - and therefore I am doing it with pleasure. I accept what is and do not get lost in unrealistic wishful thinking or bitter complaining.

Joy: If joy rather than a sense of scarcity motivates your actions, when you are doing something because you really like doing it and not primarily to get something else from it, then your work is joyful. And when you let go of judgement, you will probably enrich the lives of others in your best possible ways.

Enthusiasm: This is when you enjoy what you are doing, and at the same time find it profoundly meaningful - that it has a purpose that you really like. Enthusiasm does not trigger any resistance. It doesn´t confront. It creates no winners and losers. It often rubs off on others and is inclusive rather than exclusive. Where the ego in its efforts often tries to take, enthusiasm can give from its abundance. The ego and enthusiasm cannot exist together.

You live within a context and this is where you have to find a space suitable for living who you are. If you find it where you are, all is well, but if you realise that you have to mutilate yourself, or in other ways be unfaithful to whom you are to conform, then it is up to you to do something about it. Nobody else can live your life for you or offer you suitable circumstances without your participation. You have to speak out and communicate with your environment, or move away when you cannot accept your present situation or find any joy and enthusiasm in your life, to try to co-create a better situation together with another environment. When you are honest and outspoken with yourself, other people in your surroundings can become a little shaken up and start seeing you, learn something about how it can be to live and work under these circumstances, care about you and maybe respond to your needs. Honest and outspoken responses from your environment give you a chance to wake up and find out if there is something in your view on life that makes you unnecessarily unhappy, for example, if you are trapped in unrealistic expectations regarding what life should be. By this kind of open and honest dialogue, a new and more human society may be co-created.

When we don´t have a clear definition of the problem to start with, or when we are not quite sure about what is wrong or what a satisfying solution would look like, our habitual and well-trained goal-means-thinking doesn`t work. Instead, it is a creative process where we step by step in an ongoing dialogue are groping our way along towards a yet unknown situation, which when realised may be experienced as a satisfactory solution. It is like painting a picture, where the process of painting starts living a life on its own in the dialogue between the artist and the half-finished picture, where the inner responses of the painter on each new element in the picture guides the next step. This is where acceptance, joy and enthusiasm can be signs that you are on the right track.

Each and everyone´s experience that something feels very wrong can be used as a starting signal for co-creational processes. Through these our society can be transformed step by step until we acquire a more sustainable development coloured by love more than ego-needs.

New opportunities?

Again, we live in a continuous interplay with our environment. In the previous chapter the focus was primarily on how we need to change our own attitudes to meet the urgent need for profound transformation, where we have to formulate new goals and design new maps of reality to replace those we developed while scarcity was the prevailing problem and our main challenge was to provide as many as possible with their basic needs. But now we have surpassed many planetary boundaries. Our planet cannot take more of what we have been doing so far. So now, at the same pace that people are getting enough of their basic needs, we have to find new meaningful values to go for, work for and interchange on the global market to experience real and sustainable development. Then we have to liberate ourselves from material comparison games and the dominance of the ego to become more inner-directed. We need to replace our instrumental "I-It-relationships" to the environment with an "I-Though-attitude". In this chapter I will point at the mutuality of this interplay and ask what new possibilities the environment is offering.

Epigenetics is a fairly new science focusing on this mutuality between the individual and the environment. By studying identical twins, scientists found that twins with identical DNA can develop very different characteristics if they live in different environments. Even traits as basic as sexuality may develop in different directions where one could become a homosexual while the other is a heterosexual. It is the same phenomenon as how different the oak tree developed from an acorn planted in an open field will be from the one resulting from the same acorn planted in a rocky place. So in part it is the old question of heredity and environment that is actualised in a new form. But epigenetics works all the way down to the micro-level and are focused on both in how the genetic make-up is developed and how it is controlled. All our body cells have an identical genetic make-up, but it is the environment that determines which genes are activated and which are inactivated. Use it or lose it. Because their functions are very different, a liver cell is very different from a nerve cell or a skin cell. The same kind of influence from the environment works on higher levels as well - where we should keep in mind that we humans are each other´s environment to a great extent.

Maybe this co-creation with the environment is the natural order of nature and life. If we add the fact that cells are continually dying and replaced by new ones, so that whole body parts are renewed after a year or so (depending on what body part), we understand how dynamic life is. To follow the continuous dynamic of nature requires much more thinking in terms of processes and systems than the machine like linear goal-means-thinking that we have trained for many years, not to say generations, and have got used to. These observations have influenced much of what Peter Senge calls "learning organisations" and what is spread and put into practice around the world by the worldwide network the Society for Organizational Learning (SoL).

The baboons

One example of how an unexpected change in the environment can trigger a profound transformation of the culture in a society is that of the community of baboons described in the text that follows. Especially if we keep in mind that we, the individuals in the group, are an important part of each other´s environment.

A researcher had studied a group of baboons for decades. As is usually the case among baboons, the group was controlled by some aggressive males who were busy fighting for power with each other on one hand and harassing the females and the more peaceful males on the other. But something happened that transformed this innate culture or nature of baboons. The group found a refuse heap where they could easily collect their food. For a long time this was an excellent pantry, but one day somebody threw away meat among the refuse and this seemed to be the delicacy of the day. It was only enough for those who were the first to collect it and the greediest, who also had the sharpest elbows, were the aggressive males, all got a share of the meat. What nobody knew was that the meat was poisonous. So all the aggressive males died leaving the females and the decent and peaceful males behind them. Without the aggressive males they developed an entirely new and peaceable culture. Suddenly the baboons were much kinder to each other. And they seemed to like the new order. They had discovered new possibilities that they did not know existed and the decent males were allowed to mate and pass on their peaceable genes, which they could not before. When the representatives of the law of the strongest were not there to nourish the brutal culture, the new and peaceful ones could get more and more established.

To prevent inbreeding, the group needed new blood from outside. Therefore, nature had seen to it that sexually mature males left their childhood companions to capture a group of their own. So when a potential conqueror came to try his luck with our little group, he expected that the usual laws of the strongest would prevail. Accordingly, he started with his most impressive series of aggressive demonstrations to provoke his rivals to try to fight him, hoping to conquer them and take over leadership. At the same time, he hoped that the ladies would be impressed and charmed by his strength, but he got no response. The decent and peaceful guys had no desire to fight, so he was standing there alone shouting and waving his arms in vain, feeling more and more ridiculous. And the ladies were not impressed at all, so instead the new male had to become more humble and start studying what rules and norms prevailed in this special group, how they lived together and how he could make himself welcome. Somehow, this newly developed culture must also have been attractive to other baboons, because aggressive males from outside were continually willing to adapt to the conditions of this group. The peaceful culture could persist in spite of frequent attacks. The outsiders must have been happily surprised by the attractive opportunities they could experience in this peaceful and more loving co-existence.

Who knows, maybe the climate threat corresponds to the poisonous meat breaking the dominance of the habitual orders in society, giving room for entirely new ways of living together that might show up as much more attractive as soon as they have had a chance to establish themselves and be experienced by many enough people in our society.

Laws and ethics

Another dividing line between the exercise of power, fear and exterior guidelines on one hand and love and interior guidelines on the other is the one between law and ethics. The law (and thereby society) comes between the perpetrator and the victim. The crime is seen as a crime against the law rather than as a violation of the individual. The perpetrator and the victim do not need to meet personally, but only via words of an act that both parties try to use at their advantage. While the aim of the law is to settle whether something wrong has been done according to given rules and laws, ethics has quite another starting point. Ethics is about our willingness and courage to see, acknowledge and accept responsibility for our dark and destructive sides and admit that we are greedy, jealous, aggressive and revengeful, but also that we are able to love something more than our self-interest and that we are willing to protect what we love (another person, nature, fair play, honesty, self respect, a clean enough consciousness) against our greedy and aggressive impulses.

Ethics has nothing to do with punishment and reward. It is not about norms and it is not nourished by fear but by love. It is born out of the dilemma that what I love and want to protect is threatened by me trying to get something that I desire; that I take at the cost of others. There is no absolute given right or wrong, but our ethical sensibility is nourished and developed by our wrestling with the ethical dilemmas we meet in our everyday life. In contrast to law, ethics has no person in authority and no one obeying. Each one of us is responsible for our own actions and nobody can make out commandments and lists of what are sins and duties for others. We have to have ourselves as our starting point and ask ourselves *What would I do and how would I think and feel if what I am up to is about my child, my brother or my mother?* While law looks for guidance from outside, ethics looks inward by being aware of what thoughts, feelings and impulses to act are awoken by the actual situation.

But wrestling with ethical dilemmas can be demanding, painful and revealing. We have to admit the shameful temptations we are wrestling with, at least to ourselves. Without guidance from outside, we have to trust our own judgement. The more we believe that there is a "right" answer, the more we fear that our confusion is a revealing sign of disgraceful deficiencies in our ability to feel empathy or love. In an effort to avoid these trials we ask for ethical rules that others have agreed upon to hide behind. But: use it or lose it! Skills and abilities that we don't use will easily wither away. Those who have taken part in formulating ethical rules have had a chance to try their ethical sensibility, but those who only want to follow already formulated rules run the risk of losing their empathic skill. They are more focused on "not doing wrong" than "doing something good". Innate abilities must be used and practiced to be kept alive.

People who dare to think for themselves, who are more focused on doing something good than avoiding making mistakes is what the world needs today. We need to train for a much higher level of inner direction than we needed in the industrial society. Wrestling with ethical dilemmas is an excellent training arena where everyday life offers many cases to practice.

For example, at a ward for dialysis they were confronted by the question whether they should continue giving dialysis to patients who had become so old and demented that they neither understood what the dialysis was good for, nor recognised the nurses who had taken care of them for several years. To continue treatment was to block this resource for somebody else needing it. To stop giving dialysis would be to stop a life-sustaining treatment. It is easy to understand that this is a very traumatic decision to make, especially for those who have known the patient since he was young and full of life. It is also easy to understand the temptation to pass on the decision to the chief of the clinic or the politicians. Then we have easier to justify ourselves by blaming the decision of somebody else, but if we do not agree with the decision and still have a living consciousness, then we remain with the ethical conflict of doing something that we dislike and do not believe in. What is the inner cost of carrying these kinds of unsolved conflicts and tensions? And is this way of passing one´s own responsibility on to somebody else something that develops the responsible, sensitive, independent people that we need at the most in today's society?

In the dialysis ward, nobody was allowed to run away from the dilemma. Instead the staff got help in working through their ethical conflicts by sharing them with their colleagues on regular ethical rounds. They were encouraged to be open and honest about their feelings and thoughts about the situation, instead of being yes men or trying to argue to convince each other of the best solution. By sharing the emotional storms and their irresolution by staying in the creative void together, a sensible way of dealing with the situation emerged out of the confusion.

Ethics is less about finding the "right" solutions than letting yourself get emotionally touched by the ethical conflict you are facing, meeting that instead of running away. It is primarily by dramatic events that we become aware of what is important to us; what has more value than our self-interest. It is by wrestling with the ethical dilemma, where one value only can be won at the cost of another important value that the ethical sense is kept alive and is developed. And it is by accepting the challenge of these wrestling matches that ethical self-esteem and pride is strengthened.

Especially challenging and mentally improving is to meet another person whom I have hurt in my greediness or other selfishness face to face. For example, where a perpetrator, with the help of a mediator, meets his victim. The victim gets a chance to make clear what costs the crime has caused, emotional and otherwise - often of quite another kind than material loss, which is the gain for the perpetrator. The perpetrator gets a chance to take responsibility for what he has done. These meetings are painful for both parties. Both fear them. But those who dare to go through the meeting usually experience it as both relieving and enriching, especially compared to what it was like carrying around the fantasies and undirected feelings that they had before the meeting. Mediation is arranged only after the verdict has fallen, so it does not affect the sentence at all. The aim is to finish off the event emotionally and personally.

Most adolescents who receive an offer of mediation are willing to meet their victims in spite of their fear and sense of discomfort associated with it. The wish to take responsibility seems to be quite strong after all, at least as long as it is used and is not blunted. It is by meeting each other face to face that reconciliation is possible, and accepting a personal responsibility can promote self-respect and pride. So victims who are willing to meet up for mediation are doing a healing job when the perpetrator is brave enough to face up to an "I-Thou meeting". I believe that it means much more than severe punishment. The victim has a chance to transform desire for revenge into a conciliatory meeting, which can make it easier to let the painful crime pass into history.

The conditions for success is the mutuality, that all parties involved are willing to meet, listen to each other and try to really understand the other´s perspective - a real I-Thou-meeting. Such a personal meeting probably makes it easier to understand the reason for the sentence and to accept it. But if one of the parties refuses mediation, one is at the mercy of the law. For many perpetrators this can feel like being left at the mercy of a superior congregation of people that are seen as a different sort, and to be an object to their judgements and argumentation, "I-It". The risk is great that the trial will be coloured much more by bitterness than reconciliation and that the punishment is experienced as injustice. At the same time an irreconcilable victim almost always demands a harsher punishment to make up for the pain they have suffered in the belief that a massive retaliation will lessen the pain in the old spirit of a vendetta: An eye for an eye; a tooth for a tooth.

An ethical forum at every place of work

Our emotional responses, empathy and compassion are important and natural resources in our interaction with the environment. They give life and mutuality to the interplay. If we don´t use them we will become deformed as humans in the long run and become robots, ice-cold bureaucrats or greedy businessmen. The ethical sensibility and the ability to love is something that needs practice to be kept alive and to develop, for example, by wrestling with ethical dilemmas. If we want to keep people´s ethical attitude alive, and if we want to make use of a wholehearted engagement and responsibility from our staff, an ethical forum at every place of work would be of extreme value. It would be a forum where employees have an opportunity to give air to their doubts, thoughts and emotions, their confusion or irresolution, their feeling of powerlessness. Maybe this would also affect stress, sick leave and staff turnover. It is a strain on one's nerves and health to carry around unsolved conflicts without opportunity to share them with others or to be forced to shut off one's feelings in order to stand the situation.

An ethical forum is different from traditional problem solving discussions, where you are looking for solutions to defined problems. This is more about meeting around difficult situations to share each other's different experiences and reactions to them, to stay with them long enough to reflect on them and maybe learn something from them, with no special expectations of what the meeting should result in. The focus is to keep the ethical issues alive and to train our ethical sensibility by showing in practice that they are taken seriously. By this form of contact, we become clearer about what we really find important and valuable and what we find less important. What are the core values that we want to protect and nourish for the future? What can we let go of? These reflections and dialogues will probably touch our hearts and affect us as persons and our way of living our private life, as well as our work life and social life.

In your work you may be confronted by situations that are especially upsetting and difficult to manage. The opportunity to bring these out at an ethical forum with a supportive and non-judgemental climate can help you to really feel and let yourself be touched as a whole human being. At an ethical forum you can get comfort, support and new inspiration. Others may have met a similar situation as yours and can recognise their own reactions in yours. Or maybe they reacted in another way and found a satisfactory solution to the dilemma. If we dare to be open and honest with our emotions, agonies and difficulties, we can be excused from going around thinking that we are the only ones feeling confused and that no-one else has difficulties in managing the situation. By sharing what actually *is* we can escape from feeling not good enough according to more or less unrealistic ideals and conceptions of how things should be or could be. We learn more about what it is to be a human being to a full extent at our work. We can get confirmation and respect for the ethical dilemmas that our work is confronting us with. And when they become visible they might also be possible to act on.

These kinds of ethical dialogues can be initiated from different angles and by different needs. People may want to give a special event an airing among colleagues and supervisors. People from different companies may want to gather to have ethical dialogues around a special dilemma facing a whole branch. Where there are recurrent collisions of interest, it might be a good idea to gather the parties involved to a dialogue to try to find an ethical solution to the situation. Bureaucratic rules may have such devastating secondary effects that all perspectives involved may want to deal with in collaboration from the ground. There are many kinds of ethical dilemmas, where something that I love is threatened by something else that I also desire, but which are not compatible.

Ethical dialogues can have many different forms, more or less spontaneous or well organised and magnificent:
- Descriptions of common ethical dilemmas that are part of the profession can be gathered on small pieces of paper in a pot. Then at coffee breaks and the like,

one can randomly take one of the papers and have a discussion about what experience the people at the table have had of this dilemma. The stock of dilemmas can be filled in by other´s experiences of interesting dilemmas.

- A consultant can support the parties involved to have a dialogue, "I-Thou", around some actual collision of interest or ethical dilemma that each of them is involved in. It can be when only two persons are involved or whole work groups or groups from several departments.
- The organisation can arrange seminars with representatives from several stakeholders whose different perspectives would be of value for the solution of certain dilemmas in relation to them.
- A branch organisation may want to gather representatives from many member companies to try out how certain ethical dilemmas facing the branch can be managed.
- An ethical dialogue can be suggested by anyone feeling a need for it. Or one can arrange regular meetings with an open space where the participants can suggest what ethical dilemmas they want to bring out for a dialogue.

So, an ethical forum can have many forms. The important thing is to devote some time and a place for wrestling with ethical dilemmas. It is also important to develop forms for the meetings to ensure that they are experienced as safe and inspiring enough to make the participants willing to open themselves to each other, and to find a structure that is supportive in helping them to get in contact with their ethical dilemmas. The way of talking to each other is crucial for making the meetings meaningful and enriching enough to be experienced as worth keeping alive.

Dialogue is not discussion and arguing. It is less about finding the right answer than about wrestling together with the dilemmas and living them through to experience a personal stance. The aim is to develop and practice a way to meet and manage ethical inner conflict by really listening to each other´s different perspectives and respecting each other´s experience as their truth at this moment, as a piece of fact, "I-Thou". All too often, these kinds of gatherings degenerate into endless discussions about how it should be and arguments about right and wrong. We result-oriented Westerners are unaccustomed to stay with "what is" in the process and let the answers emerge out of that. We are more trained to think in terms of goal-means or problem-solution and find it frustrating to stay in the creative void and the irresolution prevailing there. But more discussion clubs are not what we need. There are plenty of those offered by political, religious and other interest groups.

The ethical consciousness that I want to promote by meeting in ethical forums is about an inner process. It is about practicing the sensitivity for ethical dilemmas and the ability to live them through, rather than talking about them as objects outside oneself. As a psychotherapist, I can´t tell my clients how they should live their lives, that is their business. In the same way we can´t prescribe how people should experience and manage an ethical dilemma, but we can support them by accompanying them while they are wrestling with their agony, confusion and irresolution while searching their way forward step by step. We can listen, ask for clarity, share our own experiences when listening, confirm, challenge and, as a speaking partner, help them to clarify their own stance and base it on a richer reality seen from different perspectives - like a coach supporting his adept in using their inborn resources.

As the I-Thou-dialogue is far from granted in our goal-directed culture, some initial help might be requested to start an ethical forum. A consultant who is used to leading dialogue can be of great help until many enough of the participants have experienced the meaning of dialogue to bring the conversation back to I-Thou when it starts to degenerate into "talking about" opinions and other kinds of discussions and argumentations. Gestalt has quite a lot to offer here, as I-Thou contact and mindfulness are two of its cornerstones. Gestalt therapists or consultants have four years of practice of I-Thou dialogue in their training, but there are also other process consultants working with dialogue as one of their most important tools.

Authenticity is always touching

One important intention of setting up an ethical forum is to create a training arena where people can practice their empathic ability and compassion by using them - you know, use it or lose it. In a world marked by a striving for superficial, controllable and measurable measures of progress of the personal value as well as of the value of one´s work, the risk is otherwise great that these abilities will wither away from a lack of application. But entrepreneurship from the heart is what is most needed today. It is those who don´t bother about living up to other´s measures of success, and who stop playing roles in order to follow their inner voice instead, who can introduce the new consciousness and change the world. They can see with their eyes and feel with their heart. They can perceive phenomena that are not put in the prevailing maps of reality. They dare to stand up for who they are and can openly and honestly express their experiences without furtively glancing at others to control what is the proper opinion. Those are the people who open new perspectives - also for others. In the long run they are the ones who gain the respect of others, who will listen to them. Not only your surroundings but also you yourself feel good by authenticity. According to my experience as a therapist for a large number of therapy groups what is most healing is the opportunity to show yourself exactly as you are and be seen and received in this in a supportive, honest, respectful and non-judgemental way. Where surrounding people can react honestly and openly with negative feelings or spontaneous thoughts and fantasies. Where their responses are not heard as judgements or objective truths, but as declarations of fact: "This is how I react. Here I am." What triggers irritation is very seldom what people actually show of themselves, even if that is shameful or troublesome and the person was afraid of showing from the beginning. What evokes irritation is almost always when people are trying to hide what is obvious to others or when they are attempting to make things better than they are.

This is quite logical: To dare to show also shameful parts of myself is an act of confidence and an invitation to others to openly be themselves as well. To show only a beautiful surface is an act of distrust against others, not trusting their ability to tolerate reality as it is or their conciliatory love. Then I see them as potential bullies and we ruin the opportunity to be realistic mirrors of each other and to take part of the other´s perspective, thereby widening our own world and learn from each others.

The aim of an ethical forum is to give us an opportunity to take part in each other´s ethical perspective, as ethics is something profound and personal regular meetings in an ethical forum can train the ability to create a safe, honest and open climate. This is an ability that is most valuable everywhere we want or need to take part of each other´s different perspectives.

A holistic view based on many perspectives

Things look different from different perspectives. When you look at a table straight from above, you notice certain features of it, which are different from those you can see from the side or from underneath. In spite of the differences, no perspective is truer than another. They are just different aspects of the table. To get a more holistic view of what kind of a table it is, you have to combine the perspectives and add some more: Can you sit by it without banging your knees into it? Is the surface heat or water-resistant? And there may be other features that require special knowledge to recognise, before you can tell for what you can use it and if you like it or not.

From our different personal histories and experiences we have formed different views of the world, different maps of reality. From our different positions and missions in society and at work, different phenomena emerge as relevant and important, while others pass by unnoticed. Our wish to do good and find real meaning in what we are doing can make us stand there with our "hammer waiting for the nails to emerge". You will notice that I am back at the old issue of map and terrain, and to a great extent we deal with reality through our maps of it.

From the top of the mountain you have the wide view. You can see other mountains, forests, lakes and rivers, roads, farms and villages in the landscape. Fields of flowers are perceived as colourful surfaces. But if you want to know how the flowers smell, you have to be on the ground where they grow. From there you can also see if they look healthy or not, see the humidity of the soil and a lot of other details that you can´t see from the top of the mountain. And in the forest you can listen to the birds living there, study where and how they are building their nests, etc. But from there you can´t see the forest because of all the trees. So, to get a holistic view of life on and around the mountain, everybody has to be willing to share their perspective with others and to listen to and acknowledge their perspectives. If you want to co-create life-promoting conditions on and around the mountain, firstly you have to agree on what kind of life you want to promote. Then you can tell each other what you have seen from your different points of view affecting these qualities positively or negatively, and how the influence is created. Then you have a basis for action.

Aren't companies and organisations in a similar situation, trying to create favourable conditions for life where they are working? Where they step by step in a co-creative interplay with the environment are trying to find a mutual exchange that is as positive as possible for both the company and its surroundings. Those who want to have a holistic view have the same need to take care of all perspectives involved, especially if we need to create new maps and new measures of progress, where the economic one-sidedness in the established ones are becoming more and more obsolete. (See "Development by interplay with the surroundings", page 31 ff)

At the same time, democratic and technical developments are offering better and better opportunities to take care of different perspectives. The development of modern IT is an example. While working with Work Ethics around 1975, the way in which computerisation was more or less forced onto the companies caught my interest. Most of the data systems were designed to suit the need for overview by the management, while those who were feeding in the data had very little use for it. Naturally, they were not very motivated to contribute to and work with systems that were mainly there to control and direct them. Computers were not looked upon as their tools, but rather as control-instruments of the "opponents", where the main challenge was to manipulate the system into giving favourable responses, rather than making reality more visible and transparent.

I thought that this was a misuse of a brilliant tool, and that it would be quite easy to change. The specialty of computers is to remember and very quickly process large amounts of data. So the computers could first be programmed to suit the needs of the users, who could make their best use of them. Then in a new step the original data could be taken care of more or less automatically by another program that would aggregate and categorise it to suit the needs of the management. It is much easier to aggregate the smallest elements into meaningful wholes, than to split up wholes into its parts. So instead of letting the machine-producers carry on making programs adapted to the available machines/computers and the needs of the managers who were usually those who bought the computers, I wanted to ask the users how they would like to use a tool like a computer. And where they could imagine that they would make the best use of it, if they by some magic could own such a computer. That should be the starting point for the development of programs as well as machines.

I went to IBM with the idea. I thought that Sweden, with its homogenous population, would be an excellent experimentation market that would quickly adapt to a new idea if it liked it and which would never accept anything else, if it found out that data processing could be divided up into personally adapted modules. But IBM refused the idea and said that Sweden was such a small market that they could easily take the loss if I happened to be right and somebody else would successfully try the idea. So I went to Data-Saab, the sole Swedish computer-company at that time, but they were close to bankruptcy and were closing down. Rank Xerox showed some interest, but didn´t use my ideas as far as I knew. But as these ideas were very much in line with those that Apple was based on; it was thrilling for me when I recently happened to see a TV programme about how modern IT, Apple and Macintosh started at Xerox Park where the founders of Apple, Steve Jobs and Steve Wozniak, met. Somehow the ideas were already there, but they were the only ones who really saw the potential in them and did something about it.

Of course I can´t resist enjoying the possibility that my thoughts might be the origin of Apple and modern IT. Or that it is a thrilling example of synchronicity. But my reason for telling this story from the computer world is to show how unwilling we are when it comes to letting go of a winning concept. IBM was very successful by that time and saw no reason to change, but the story also shows how rapid development can be, if we allow ourselves to think outside habitual frames. And how these two guys opened the doors for modern IT, which is now making it easier and easier to take part of each other's different perspectives. The internet is making knowledge available for everybody, which makes it possible for each one of us to see our perspective in a wider context. So the opportunities to make use of different perspectives are growing at the same time as the reasons for doing so are growing, while we have to co-create new sustainable measures of progress and new maps of reality.

Dialogue as a tool

In the section "By machine-thinking we become servants to our tools" (page 24 ff) I pointed out the risk of becoming slaves to our tools. We are more anxious about maintaining and keeping our tools intact than we are concerned about visioning the world and work that we want to create and then developing the tools that could help us realise our visions. But now I realise that I emphasise dialogue as the most important tool for almost everything that I am dealing with in this book. Am I a slave under the tool that I have practiced the most and am comfortable with, leading dialogue? Am I sitting here with my "hammer" looking for "nails" where I can use it?

Perhaps that is the case. I only pay attention to problems that are not (yet) well defined. Problems that are clear, well-specified and can be organised in chains of goal-means can be very well solved by programmes and plans, like a machine. The solution can even be automatised. These cases don´t demand very much dialogue, but to agree on the goal or the problem and specify cause-effect-relationships often requires both research and dialogue, or at least an intense exchange of information. After having clearly defined the problem, we are often enormously efficient. In their book *The Necessary Revolution*, Peter Senge et al. describe a couple of very impressive examples of how companies, often in co-operation, have been very successful in eliminating almost all pollution by using waste from one process as input to another and in using other kinds of recycling. But in spite of these technical successes, the main part of the book is about how we can affect the social systems that by ignorance, unconsciousness, greediness, carelessness, short sightedness or whatever are disturbing the natural ecological systems that would otherwise regulate the needs of nature in an organic way.

To accept available knowledge also requires dialogue, especially if it challenges the status quo. For example, there is still a group of people who doubt that the present climate threat is caused by human activity or who even deny the existence of a climate threat as such, although there is consensus about this among a vast majority of scientists. And truly, those who long for a transformation of our way of living, and like the idea that the climate threat is forcing us into such a change, are unwilling to question the conclusions of the researchers. Others may have stronger reasons for doing so.

To get hold of and make use of a growing mass of knowledge may also require some dialogue. When my grandfather was young, electricity was new. He could study to become an art historian, an architect and an electrical engineer. One brain could contain all the knowledge available. About twenty-five years ago I asked a medical professor who specialised in the study of ears if he knew a colleague in Stockholm whom I also knew. He answered, "I know who he is, but we don´t have much to do with each others as he is working with the inner ear, while I am working with the outer ear." The available knowledge was of such a large quantity that it had to be split into sub-specialties such as outer-ear and inner-ear. So when we face the challenge of describing what systems are involved in the problems of sustainability and what we can do about them, we can imagine what an enormous amount of information is needed to find and combine all relevant knowledge. Here we have to gather people with different perspectives and different knowledge to combine their knowledge and creativity into a collective super-brain. And that requires interdisciplinary dialogue.

Often change processes are designed as a relay race with sequential steps 1, 2, 3 etc being passed on from one actor to the next until the goal is reached. This is how a machine is designed and it is applicable when you have a clear chain of goal-subgoals and reality lies still like a track while you are running from goal to goal. But an organisation is more like a living organism. It will react to each attempt to change it. And people can react differently to the same activity from outside depending on how they perceive the initiative to change, how it will affect them and their work, and whether they like change processes or not. Therefore, different steps may have to be taken in parallel and you have to be flexible and sensitive to what is happening in the interaction. Working with change in organisations is like a soccer game where the team members need to know each other´s peculiarities quite well. And as this is not a win/lose-game, but rather a way to learn and practice change-processes, you also want to take part of as much as possible of the perceptions and experiences of all who are involved in the process. Again, there is a need for dialogue.

In her 2009 thesis,[9] Eva Amundsdotter reports how she tried to change the culture in a couple of schools to develop more genuine gender equality. Usually the existence of inequality was denied or unnoticed. So in Eva´s strategy to create more awareness of the real situation, the "development-process" is central. She starts with different observed episodes and stays with them together with those involved to reflect on what more or less unnoticed norms and assumptions that are taken as given and are passively accepted as premises for the

---

9 Att framkalla och förändra ordningen, Luleå Tekniska Universitet 2009.

episodes. In this way, she lets the underlying system of norms gradually emerge, like a photo develops in its development-bath. Not until the system of norms has shown itself in this way, will the "mobilisation" and "change-processes" start. So especially when we have to move away from habitual patterns that might be based on norm-systems that are unconsciously taken as given, dialogue is important. And isn´t this exactly the situation, when we have to change from doing more of what we have been doing until now to doing something entirely different without knowing what? There is a lot that we have taken as given and have to liberate ourselves from.

The more we move away from habitual thought-patterns and given structures, the more important dialogue is in the change-process. As long as we are satisfied with technical solutions to minimise pollution, our habitual goal-means-thinking is all right. But the more we focus on co-creating a new sustainable life-style and world trade, the more dialogue is required. The more we look for fundamental solutions rather than symptom solutions, the more important that dialogue is.

Symptom solutions - fundamental solutions

When we have a headache it is tempting to cure it with a pill. And often that works - the headache disappears. There is a linear cause and effect relationship. But quite often the headache is a symptom of a greater underlying problem. It signals to us that there is too much stress for us at our job, that we sleep too little or are eating unhealthy food or are neglecting ourselves in other ways. If this is the case, and we are shutting this warning signal off by a pill, a symptom solution, it leaves us free to continue as before allowing the underlying problems grow and cause more serious consequences than a simple headache. So in the long run, curing the symptoms alone doesn't help us. We have to deal with the underlying reasons for the problem and look for deeper solutions.

As symptom solutions are usually much simpler and more in line with our well-trained linear goal-means-thinking than fundamental solutions, we are tempted to try them first on most of our problems. We try to push problems away from a more personal and demanding level to more neutral symptom solutions that can be quickly and easily applied by technological means. This has gone so far that in many ways we have lost our capacity to try fundamental solutions that require more I-Thou-contact with the situation at hand. We are back at the observation about the hammer and the nail, where we too hastily define problems in a way that is suitable to available solutions, rather than scrutinising their inner nature before jumping to conclusions and making decisions. We twist reality to make it match the map that we are accustomed to and feel safe with, rather than redraw the map to make it a good guide in present reality.

For a long time, technological development has been so rapid that we have become used to quickly finding technical solutions to problems. It has gone so far that we confuse progress with technological development, although it may not have contributed to greater happiness at all, but rather created more problems than it solved. For example, we go by car from door to door instead of walking or biking. Lacking physical exercise we then have to take measures to lose weight and take care of our health. Technology has made it possible for us to run faster and faster in the same tracks, but at the same pace the damage of our habitual life style has grown and accumulated.

If we don´t want to stop technological development, we have to train our ability to find fundamental solutions. We need to put in technology in its greater context and notice what has more value than something else, what is more central to life on Earth than other things. We have to take ethical dilemmas seriously and develop ourselves as mature, loving and responsible persons. To find fundamental solutions requires more of systems thinking and process thinking than we are used to with our predominant linear goal-means thinking. What processes lead to the problems? How are they related?

Development in its greater context

To balance our excessive belief in technological development, we need to train our capacity for I-Thou-contact with each other, as well as with the phenomena in our environment that we interact with. We must learn how to make use of our direct experiences in our co-creation of a desirable future - to meet in the experienced world, rather than in the map-world.

Today we trust science to a great extent and expect it to serve us solutions. But this is as misleading as it is to put all our hopes to spiritual leaders and the true faith and just swallow their beliefs as ready-made solutions. Both perspectives must be integrated if we want to take care of modern science and use it wisely in the service of life. Both can inspire us. But we cannot just accept solutions from outside and apply them without digesting them and making them our own. They require personal commitment, personal responsibility and personal choices.

But to dare to stand up for your own opinions and experiences can be difficult, especially when they are experienced as deviant. We live in and are dependent on our closest environment. To be pushed out of the community and lose the feeling of belonging can be catastrophic. At the same time, the pressure to fit in can be great. So the fear of being looked upon as odd can be realistic. Rather than challenging prevailing norms and beliefs, people keep experiencing that they are afraid and are considered abnormal to themselves.

For example, when adolescents were asked why they were smoking, they answered, "Because it's cool." On the follow up question, "Do you think it's cool?" most of them answered, "No." But as nobody dared to speak out loud about this, the idea could survive and trap youngsters into starting smoking in spite of the initial unpleasant coughing. How many adults do not keep silent in the same way of their spiritual experiences, because they are afraid of becoming ridiculed about them? What we don´t speak out about and share with others leaves a void that is quickly filled with fantasies of different kinds - both our own and those of others.

So to be a pioneer and speak your truth, always requires some courage. History gives us testimonies of this. For example, think of Galileo or dissidents from totalitarian or fundamentalist countries! But as knowledge after some time proved Galileo to be right, maybe the attitude to spiritual experiences and interest will change and encourage people to share more of this with each other. Where we can separate actual spiritual experiences that we can take personal responsibility for from old-fashioned religious superstition that we were more or less forced to swallow undigested. That we are getting used to start looking at the more mysterious quantum world as real as the Newtonian world. For a long time we have learnt and developed tools to deal with the Newtonian world, while we have only known about the quantum world for about one hundred years, leaving laymen quite untrained and without tools to deal with it. Quantum physics can help us to understand some inexplicable and unlikely spiritual phenomena, and a couple of spiritual traditions and practices might be seen as intuitive training to meet the quantum world.

To realise a transformation into a new direction we must add something more than exciting ideas, discussions and talking about. We find the seeds to real change in our own experiences that we get from our everyday life. That is why it is so important to develop trustful meeting points where we can feel safe enough to openly and honestly share our experiences with each other, however odd they may seem. It can be done through network or nourishment groups that meet for mutual inspiration. But the closer to work that these meeting places are, the shorter the distance between word and action.

For the same reason it is important to start out from our own everyday reality. To talk about global solutions may easily frighten people away and make them lose interest. Because who lives their everyday life on the global scene? No, the best for the whole is something you notice inside yourself wherever you are. To be at service of the best for the whole and to commit yourself to a desirable future is to care about what you get aware of from your point of view and to surrender to what the whole or a desirable future is demanding of you at this moment. The whole shows itself locally in its different expression. Everything is connected and a change in one part of the interrelated system spreads to throw branches to other parts. We cannot change the bigger system overnight, but we can commit ourselves to continuous development of our awareness and ability to choose.

That is why personal development is so important. It keeps you alive and alert.

Summary - new opportunities?

The awareness of the need for fundamental change is spreading. People worldwide are to a much greater extent considering sustainability and consequences for the environment in their choices - as consumers, employees or financiers. The effort to find global agreements are intensified, which in turn is increasing the global awareness which is also nourished by the possibility for everyone to find information on the internet.

The rise of ethical awareness may also increase the interest to start dialogue around ethical dilemmas. As ethics is such a deep and personal inner affair, such dialogue can practice the capacity for real I-Thou-contact. This capacity is important if we want to take care of each other's different perspectives to co-create new sustainable goals and measures of progress - to design new maps that are better in line with current reality.

Quantum physics is more than one hundred years old, but in spite of this it is not until now that it slowly and piecemeal is coming into consciousness outside the circle of physicists. New knowledge and new ways of thinking need a long time to settle, although we have used products based on them for a long time. Apart from offering new technical solutions, quantum physics is opening new doors to spiritual experiences, which may increase our consciousness and ability to look for answers inside us. This can contribute to making us more governed from within than from outside.

The group of baboons showed how real experiences of new attractive possibilities that we didn´t know of before can change deeply rooted instincts and cultural patterns. But the new patterns must then be given enough time to settle down and be ready to protect themselves from attacks from outside and resist efforts to redirect them into the old habitual order.

From words to deeds

We are aware of quite a lot. MORE is not what is most needed today. Climate change and other planetary boundaries are indicating that planet Earth cannot take more of what we are already doing. We also know that we don´t get happier by more, when we have enough to secure basic needs (www.equalitytrust.org.uk). After that, "more" is only used in our status struggle and to keep up to the standards of our group not to lose our sense of belonging. Sustainable development means something other than more of the same, but we don´t know quite what. We have to overcome our resistance to change. We need to look outside the mapped terrain, let go of habitual thought-patterns and tools in order to formulate new attractive goals and measures of progress. Apart from overcoming the fear of leaving structures, systems and methods that have served us well, and that we have become comfortable with, this requires rewiring the brain. We have to learn new things and practice new skills to deal with tasks that until now were taken care of by our spinal cord. Therefore we are seldom willing to let go of habitual patterns until we have experienced new attractive opportunities in reality and dared to believe in them.

Sustainable goals cannot be based on comparisons and competition regarding more of the same - faster, bigger, cheaper, more exclusive, latest model ... We have to break the dominance of the ego and liberate ourselves from our pre-occupation with how we appear in the eyes of others. Instead, we have to look inside ourselves to find out what we really appreciate - what makes us happy, enthusiastic, filled with life and is in line with what we want to dedicate our lives to, where we find meaning. By practicing more I-Thou-contact with "what is" here and now, we learn more and more about how we react and choose in different situations. By this conscious presence and mindfulness from moment-to-moment we become more and more aware of what we wish of our life and work in our heart of hearts.

We are living and developing by an eternal interaction with our surroundings where our needs are looking for satisfaction - and where new possibilities are awakening or creating new needs and desires. We find the needs and desires inside us. The opportunities to satisfy them are to be found in the environment. By the responses from the environment on our attempts to satisfy our needs and wishes, we get an idea of what is possible and what is not. Based on these real experiences we can design new maps of reality.

The more rigid the environment, the more individuals are forced into passive adaptation. The more the surroundings are willing to participate in mutual interaction, the more development will become a co-creation. As long as fixed authoritarian hierarchies prevailed, people were fairly willing to adjust to them. But as old authoritarian relationships are loosened up between parents-children, teachers-pupils, managers-subordinates, owners-employees, the interplay between them becomes livelier and more and more mutual. In the old authoritarian society it was possible to organise and control a company almost as a machine. This is impossible in today´s democratic society, which is based on participation and shared responsibility to a much greater extent. Organisations of today are much more alike a living organism than a machine. Especially as we need much more flexibility, creativity and personal initiatives if we are going to survive and prosper in the changeable world of today.

Even if we share the opinions above, it is not obvious how we can get from words to deeds. Doesn´t it mean too much talking and meeting? Can we afford that? Are people really willing to meet in open and honest dialogue? Are there any signs of an emergent transformation in this direction? What can we do to support that?

Can we afford that much talk?

Can we afford that much exchange of information and participation in decision-making? Don´t we have to be alert and make quick decisions to keep pace in the global competition? Yes indeed! But the question is partly how far we can compete with low-wage countries with low-price production, partly if we can make effective use of human resources without a lot of dialogue.

Jim Collins and his research team made a study in 2001 of how companies who had reached lasting (more than fifteen years) exceptional results (profits over three times more than market index) were different from comparable companies whose results were average or normal. To find out what could make a good company great the researchers demanded a pre-history of at least thirty years with average or worse results before the breakthrough from "good to great" (GtG). In the Fortune 500 list, they found eleven companies that fulfilled these criteria and could be rated as GtG companies. Data was gathered by interviews with employees in leading positions and members of the boards in the GtG companies, as well as in comparable companies that were carefully chosen. The same questions were put to everyone. From the responses, the research team tried to identify patterns that could explain the main differences between the GtG-companies and the others (a qualitative study).

Interestingly enough, what they found was contributing to the exceptional success and profitability to a high degree was the same as I have mentioned in this book as a prerequisite for a transformation into a sustainable development. What they found was the following.

The breakthrough is the result of a consistent, iterative and cumulative process:

- A breakthrough is never caused by one single event, but is always preceded by a creative period where disciplined people have devoted themselves to disciplined thought resulting in disciplined action.

Disciplined people, people who are mature and somehow want to make a difference and contribute to a better world is a key-factor:
- What was characterising the leaders was a personal humility coupled with a professional strength of will. Unlike colourful leaders who are often seen in the media, they were not at all interested in status or being celebrities. They were focused on attaining something that they were passionate about.
- First who - then what. The starting point was to gather a team of independently thinking, feeling and acting people who wanted to work together with something that they found important and meaningful. What exactly this was, was something they step by step

agreed on by open and honest dialogue - which in turn contributed to the trustful climate in the group. It was also important not to grow faster than you have the right people for.

Disciplined thinking is realistic, firm and deepening thinking:
- Meet tough reality without losing hope! It is not until you see and dare to meet reality as "it is", that you can do something about it. Where people from different parts of the business openheartedly are sharing what they are experiencing from their different points of view. Already by accepting reality as it is, something is happening. To cheat oneself with unrealistic wishful thinking is misleading.

- The hedgehog concept. (Unlike the smart fox who tries everything possible, the hedgehog sticks to one strategy in its fight with the fox - to roll itself up into a prickly ball.) Identify the intersection between where your passion is, what you can do better than anybody else in the world and the economic motor in just your business (profit per x) - and stay firmly with this in the future. If what you are doing can be done as well by somebody else, this is not where you can become a master company. The greatness is based on your ability to find a business idea of your own, based on your unique competence. That is when the breakthrough will occur.

Disciplined action where people take their own responsibility and their own initiatives to realise and refine the business idea:
- A culture of disciplined action is characterised by independent collaborators taking responsibility for improving the business in line with the hedgehog

concept and the business idea. Disciplined people need no hierarchy. Disciplined thinking needs no bureaucracy. Instead of controlling each other, everyone can wholeheartedly devote themselves to their real work.

- Technology is an accelerator. No GtG-company was based on a new revolutionary technology. They were clever in becoming aware of and making use of new technology that could improve the business, but only then. Never new technology for its own sake, or to keep up with the latest fashion.

- The flywheel. Persistently pushing a big flywheel in one and the same direction is a good metaphor for the driving force. Continuously, step by step, trying to simplify and refine the business idea in an ever deeper, more self-evident and more integrated way - to become one with it. Trying different roads when the conditions make that necessary without losing sight of the original business idea. By each push in the same direction the flywheel is moving more and more and faster and faster because of its weight. It is a cumulative process where one step is enforcing the other. This is quite different from pushing the flywheel to and fro - which is often the case when changing the managing director, in mergers, or in the hunt for making good bargains.

In a former study, *Built to Last*, Collins tried to find out what constituted lasting results. What he found was, among other things, the following:

Core values - a guiding philosophy, a central aim where passion is the driving force - and profits and cash-flows are only regarded as necessary survival conditions, not as the goal. There is a need to keep the core ideology as an anchor, a direction - but also to stimulate change and improvement in all other areas.

Focus on the process - rather than the solution. This involves building a clock, rather than telling what time it is. Building an organisation that can sustain and adapt to several generations of managers - that is the opposite of building a company around one brilliant managing director or idea. It is about continuously practicing the skills that are necessary to meet the changeable environment that the company has to interact with.

The research by Jim Collins and his team indicates that, far from being an unnecessary cost, the attitudes and dialogue that are advocated in this book are key factors for success. Apart from sharing each other's different perspectives, it is to a great extent practicing skills that are needed to be able to deal with a changeable world. Jim Collins and co. have studied real companies and their real activities. So it has nothing to do with wishful thinking or unrealistic ideology. It is reality to learn from.

IKEA - a Swedish example

A Swedish company that has been extraordinarily successful is IKEA. They have also proceeded from words to deeds. Or maybe they have rather put words on their deeds.

One reason for Ingvar Kamprad not to introduce IKEA on the stock exchange may be that he wants to keep the company away from the short sighted shareholder focus on profitability that is often prevailing there. Instead he has been able to focus on the broader **business idea**:

"To create a better everyday life for many people by offering a wide range of well-designed, functional home furnishing products at prices so low that as many people as possible will be able to afford them."[10]

Instead of participating in the status competition and comparison game, IKEA has revolted against excluding fine culture, and has instead found its own path based on simplicity and straightness in their attitude to themselves as well as to others. By on the job training, and the power of the good example walking their talk, IKEA is consciously trying to liberate itself from status and convention to be free persons. All this is documented in an internal document from 2007 called "IKEA Values", published in Anna Jonsson`s (2007) thesis *Knowledge Sharing Across Borders - A Study in the IKEA World*.

Ikea Values

Togetherness and enthusiasm
We respect each other´s efforts. We realise that we all need each other. Everyone is prepared to lend a hand.

Constant desire for renewal
A willingness to make change. In constant search for smarter solutions.

Cost consciousness
Achieving good results with small resources. Never producing a product or service without a price tag. Awareness of those little expenses which can so easily mount up. It is impossible to have a low price if you don´t have low costs. An awareness that time is money.

---

[10] Ingvar Kamprad (1976) A furniture Dealer´s Testament, Inter IKEA Systems B.V.

Willingness to accept and delegate responsibility
We must always be more than willing to accept and to delegate responsibility. Making mistakes now and again is the privilege of the dynamic co-worker - they are the ones who have the ability to put things right. We encourage those who have the desire and the courage to take responsibility.

Humbleness and willpower
The way people behave towards other people and their ideas. Consideration, respect, friendliness, generosity, sincerity, admitting your mistakes, listening to others - these are the qualities we like to encourage at IKEA. A question of taking responsibility, making the decision and having the courage to act.

Simplicity
Simple habits, simple action are part of IKEA but we must never forget to show respect for each other.

Leadership by example
Set a good example by your behaviour and thereby create a feeling of well-being and a good working environment.

Daring to be different
"Why?", "Why not?" or "Is there another way of doing this?" We encourage our co-workers to come up with unconventional ideas and to dare to try them out. At IKEA it´s always possible to test new, exciting ideas within the framework of our concepts.

Striving to meet reality
Maintaining practical connections with daily activities.

The importance of constantly being on the way
This means being more stimulated by finding ways of achieving the goal than by the goal itself. Constantly

asking ourselves if what we are doing today, can be done better tomorrow.

Fear of making mistakes
To allow people to get things wrong now and again. To encourage initiative, but with the privilege of making mistakes and putting them right afterwards.

Diversity is part of this
We encourage an environment where people of different views, age, nationality, gender and ethnic background feel welcome. We believe that a diverse workforce will improve business results, strengthen our competitiveness and make IKEA a better place to work.

Very much in line with Jim Collins' findings around exceptionally successful companies, isn´t it?! And IKEA has been successful. Year after year IKEA is ranked at the top of the lists of the employers most preferred by students. As Anna Jonsson found in her research, these values have also been very helpful in IKEA becoming established abroad - in Russia, China and Japan.

In a country as different from ours as, for example, China, we can´t just step in and do as we do in Sweden. We must use our curiosity and interest in who the client is: What is a beautiful and well-furnished home for you? What level of self service is OK for you? What are you willing to pay for a higher degree of service? We must find out what unique competences IKEA has: What kind of resources are especially useful in satisfying the requirements from these kinds of customers? This includes everything from technical solutions to open and honest communication and pleasant behaviour. What is a pleasant behaviour in this culture and which are the traps for us? To be able to answer these kinds of questions we have to take care of all co-workers observations from their different contact points with the strange culture.

IKEA also takes part in contributing to sustainable development. For example, China is an important supplier to IKEA. About 22% of everything that IKEA sells is supplied by more than 350 Chinese companies. IKEA is putting quite an effort in supporting these to live up to IKEA´s code of conduct "Iway", that is its guidelines for taking environmental and social responsibility. Not only by using its power-position to put demands on the suppliers, but rather by establishing long term relations trying to create a mutual exchange of information and support with everything from dialogue to education programs and technical solutions. Another example is when IKEA refused to submit to corrupt systems in Russia and gave up the idea of opening a new big shop rather than paying the bribes demanded by local authorities. So here IKEA is consciously using its size in a constructive way.

If a sustainable development means a radical transformation where we have to try both unknown and untried tracks, are we not in a situation rather similar to that of IKEA from the countryside of Sweden trying to establish itself in China?! IKEA can - and is enjoying it. So why wouldn´t the rest of us be able to do it? Especially if we learn from already existing examples.

Higher Ambitions

Recent research in collaboration between Harvard Business School and Chalmers in Gothenburg verifies that there is no conflict between social responsibility and profitability, on the contrary. When social responsibility is a central part of the business idea, more employees like to go to their jobs and are proud of their employer, it is easyer to recruit good people and the employees get more energy. The research also invalidates the myth that social responsibility would be reserved for Scandinavian or enlightened American business firms. Instead, just that is what is common for exceptionally successful leaders from Sweden as well as from South Europe and India. Successful leaders also seemed to be in more active contact with their female part of their personality than others. All this is shown in the book Higher Ambitions – how great leaders create economic and social value.[11]

Mature people

According to Collins, the starting point for exceptionally successful companies is a couple of independent, mature persons who want to do something together. First who - then what. When we talk about mature people, we mean conscious and whole persons who are not unconsciously driven by their egos. Confucius acknowledged this in 500 BCE, "If you want to become a leader, you have to be a real human being. You must recognise the true meaning of life before you can become a great leader. You must understand yourself first."

The four year training run by the Gestalt Academy of Scandinavia to train Gestalt psychotherapists and Gestalt consultants is designed in a "Confucian pattern": The first two years are about I, I-Thou, I-You-We. First, understand yourself! Not until then, in the last two years, does the real practice of the profession start. The aim is to develop mature, whole persons who are able to take part in and create I-Thou-relationships, before working with other people as therapists, consultants and leaders.

---

11 Michael Beer, Tobias Fredberg et alt (2011), Harvard Business Review Press. www.higherambitions.org

But at the same time as it is very rewarding, personal development can be perceived as quite intrusive and challenging. Therefore to get some experience of what they are entering, a prerequisite for joining the education is a basic course of four residential meetings, each of which lasts four days, once every six weeks or so extended over about half a year as a preparation. The course is residential to enable those studying be able to bathe in the warm and nourishing climate that is usually developed here. Stretched out over six months, the course gives opportunities of trying new insights in everyday life and offers a safe place to return to for support, nourishment, and perhaps comfort, long enough to give eventual changes a chance to be noticed and settle down. The idea of group therapy is that it will hopefully help create a better everyday life.

The first four day meeting is dedicated to getting the group together and creating a safe and trusting atmosphere. We try to make the implicit explicit and start dealing with the issues that are most naturally in the air at this stage of the group: What kind of group is this? Who are you and why are you here? What resources are there in this group - differences/similarities, challenge/support, openness/secrecy, men/women, young/old, etc? How do I feel being in this group now? Is there anything that I can do to feel better? To be able to answer these questions we must show ourselves to each other - and are at the same time answering questions like: Who am I? How do I look upon myself today and how are others seeing me? What am I the most happy about in my everyday life - and which are my main challenges? What do I hope for in this group? What is the worst thing that could happen? Or that will not happen? Apart from creating a clearer starting point for therapy, what means the most in this first meeting is usually to feel seen and accepted by the others and the close and warm atmosphere that is created by this - to recognise ourselves in each other and share what it is to be human, in spite of living very different kinds of life.

The theme of the second group meeting is how we became who we are - how our childhood has formed us. What experiences from my childhood still colour my life? By "family constellations"[12] we can become aware of what roles in the family system we have unconsciously taken in our urge to heal the order of love in the system; to prevent anyone from being left out or forgotten by one reason or another. In different ways we try to raise the awareness of the differences between what we learned about life THEN as dependent children and what is possible NOW as adults with much better abilities to say yes and no, to move away from unwanted conditions and to reflect on our lives in their present context. We help our clients to finish unfinished business and make it up with what has already been, in order to take over the responsibility for our lives and how we want to live as adults from now on.

The third meeting is often devoted to relationships. Love relationships, sensuality and sexuality, male and female experiences, the longing for closeness and the fear of it. But often we also deal with relationships in the group. At this stage, the group members are often in a kind of teenager phase, occupied by power struggles of different kinds - with the leaders and with each other. They are struggling with questions such as: Do you still like me although I am different from you? Can I be open and honest with you without risking our relationship - so that we can create a real I-Thou-relation? What can I do

---

12 Bert Hellinger.

to contribute to this? The I-Thou-relationship is the core of both good love-relations and other close relations.

During the fourth and final meeting we deal with life-death-meaning. What is important in my life in the light of death? How would I change my life, if I had only five years left to live? Five weeks left? How do I imagine my funeral? Who will come - different groups? What will they say about me and my life? What are the different impressions of me in different groups? If my closest friend keeps a heartfelt and honest speech, what is s/he saying? Is there anything special that s/he would have wished me more or less of in my life? What is written on my gravestone as a summary of who I was? Learning from this fantasy, how do I want to live the rest of my life?

And finally it´s time to finish. Everybody meets everybody one to one to say goodbye and to thank each other for what they each have learnt from the other.

In order to create I-Thou-dialogues we support the participants in moving away from talking about to real experiences of the actual theme. We can use guided fantasies as an inner film. We can express ourselves in a picture, by movement, dance, role play, tears and laughter. We can listen to different kinds of music and let ourselves be carried away by that, and notice what comes up from our inner hiding-places - feelings, images, memories, bodily reactions, impulses to action, or other experiences. We can let our bodies speak freely to us; lie down and breathe deeply and just be with our bodies not trying to control them, letting what is coming up from our inside come. We can listen to our inner processes, while a guide takes care of the outer world. I-Thou-dialogues cannot be kept only from head to head. We also need to involve them from heart to heart in a meeting between two or more whole people. So training I-Thou-dialogues, also involves the practice of experiencing.

This is an example of how I, as a Gestalt therapist, have supported people in wrestling with their lives in a way that hopefully helps them to mature as responsible self-reliant human beings. I am proud of how progressive Gestalt has been. From having been a rebellious more or less underground therapeutic school, many of the other therapy schools are developing in the same direction. For example cognitive behavioural therapy (CBT), which is the dominant therapy school today, is based on our well-trained goal-means thinking, where you first agree on what the symptoms of the experienced problems are and then try to cure the symptoms by reprogramming unsound thought patterns. But lately, at least in Sweden, CBT has incorporated mindfulness among its main tools, calling the therapy dialectical behavioural therapy (DBT). And as they say themselves, mindfulness means that you have to let go of all striving = goal-means-thinking. Here they are approaching Gestalt, and they are heartily welcome. Psychoanalysis has incorporated the concept of mentalisation and developed "mentalisation based therapy" (MBT) leading in the same direction. So never mind what we call it. There are many good ways in which to support personal development, and many excellent courses are offered on the market. My main point is that co-workers who are by themselves looking for personal development are a strong asset for companies who want to learn from Collins´ research or the example of IKEA, or who share my views on what could contribute to a sustainable development.

Personal development by I-Thou-contact

The I-Thou-contact with what you meet in the world may be at the core of what is meant by mature and whole human beings. That you dare to stand up for a personal relationship with what you are meeting, where both body and soul, thoughts and feelings are engaged. If the thought of participating in any kind of personal development or therapy is considered as too strange or provocative, the experience of I-Thou-contact can spring up or be brought about in many other ways.

I have already mentioned the idea of forming an ethical forum at every workplace with those who in one way or another are experiencing ethical dilemmas in their work and feel forced to do something that they don´t believe in or dislike, or who are already having a personal relationship with what they are doing. They care and are touched by what they are experiencing. If they are longing to share their hesitations with others, an ethical forum is a natural meeting place. Others may not have reflected very much about what they are doing or contributing to by their work, but wake up when they are pulled into an ethical argument. If they are asked about their opinion about the issue at hand, and on what experiences they base this, they may start to develop an I-Thou-relation to the issue and want to participate in a dialogue around it.

For some people, an ethical forum seems too strange and artificial, but they may become very upset or engaged in some organisational change, an appointment of a new manager or some other event that affects themselves or a colleague. Gossip starts escalating and living its own life in the corridors. Suddenly, opposing groups are formed fighting each other. To prevent this from going too far, they may ask for a consultant to help them to solve the conflict, but although they may agree that they need a consultant, they may have different expectations on what kind of a consultant they want.

Some people might be hoping for a wise consultant solving the conflict for them by deciding what is right and what is wrong. But if they phone my wife Barbro or somebody else at her company Gestalthuset, what they get is support in solving the conflict themselves by understanding the situation better from all perspectives involved. At the same time they are given an opportunity to practice an I-Thou-dialogue that both develops them as people and is a tool that they can use in the future to solve conflicts together or deal with other common problems. She is teaching them to fish - rather than giving them a fish.

The design is the following:

1. Dialogue-based analysis of how things are at present. This is to take care of all perspectives involved. The consultants have a dialogue with each one from the client company. This is more than an interview. The aim of the dialogue is really to understand how the other is thinking, feeling and experiencing the situation and the consultant is using himself as an important tool. It is an I-Thou-meeting giving the interviewee an experience of being seen and respected.
2. The information from the interviews is put together by each one of the interviewers. Together they then compile the material into more whole and perceptible pictures of each perspective.
3. The consultants reflect on the gathered observations. What patterns do they see? What does these say about the situation? What unfinished conflicts or events need to be finished before anything else can be done? What

steps can we take after that? As the consultants have often interviewed one group each, they often represent the different perspectives involved and carry the conflicts and tension in their bodies. So already here very often an interesting parallel process emerges where the consultants can experience and explore the actual tensions and sensitivities in the organisation.
4. After having presented the whole picture and the reflections from the consultants for the client, all parties gather again to get the same information, which is always given orally. The participants are grouped into small groups to reflect on the information together. Do they recognise themselves in the picture? Is there anything they want to change or add? What do they say about the consultants´ interpretation of the situation and proposition to proceed? Decisions are made here whether to stop or proceed.

If they choose to proceed with the support of the consultants, the next step is to deal with the relationships in the group and resolve unfinished business:
5. They meet in pairs with supervision from a consultant, who supports them in keeping a real I-Thou-dialogue. They meet around issues such as: What am I especially appreciating in my interaction with you? Is there anything that I would wish more or less of? Is there anything left itching between us that needs to be finished?

This means a lot of dialogue and thereby supervised training in I-Thou-contact. You might think that this would cost many consultant hours, but then you should notice how these honest I-Thou-meetings around real and important issues can improve personal relations, the work climate and the skill in future problem solving compared to what you get out from sending the same personnel on a course. After this dialogue, the ground is prepared for other steps forward, which is to create visions together and take other steps to develop the company and to keep the engagement in finding creative contributions to a sustainable development alive.

This is very much of personal development, but you never need to mention the word - nor education, training, supervision, coaching - or even dialogue if that can be considered as provocative. We meet the client where s/he is around issues that are urgent to deal with for the client. Then it is the consultant´s way of dealing with this that gives the I-Thou-training.

Even if the solution of the actual problem is important, maybe the most permanent and valuable effect of the contribution from the consultant is the competence in I-Thou-meeting that has been trained and established in the client organisation. On the way the consultants have been dealing with the problem at hand and the clients have gained concrete experiences of what I-Thou-contact can give. They have experienced new attractive ways of being together and have been practicing this with their own real problems as their case. In order for this to happen, it is important that the I-Thou-contact is practiced naturally by the consultants. That they walk their talk and are good examples without even having to talk about it. They let go of prestige and ego, in order to be themselves instead and use their own person as a valuable instrument. Those who find this way to be an attractive opportunity and want to learn more can, for example, join the Organisational branch of the Gestalt training.

This consulting process with the management team of an international wholesale trade company, which had to deal with a very difficult transition to new owners, was studied by an independent researcher. In her interviews the managing director said, "Without this support we would not have survived the crisis. Now it has turned into a developing learning process instead of a splitting and destroying experience." According to the informants, the participating managers, the main effects of the intensive I-Thou-dialogues were the following:

Improved wholesome understanding of the company
- A shared picture and understanding of where the company is here and now.
- A shared vision of the future both for the company and the management team.
- By finishing unfinished business these could be left to history and energy freed to deal with actual reality.
- A shared understanding of how the group is working, its strengths and need for improvements.

More open and close relationships with each other.
- Greater experience of security nourished a greater sense of responsibility. The focus changed to "what can we affect" - from grumbling about unfair conditions given from others. From being angry and hurt victims, to being responsible actors.
- Synergy and collaboration across the boundaries apart from the meetings in the management team.
- Shared responsibility for the whole company.
- They could finish unfinished business on a personal level and free locked energy.
- Better focus in their meetings and some improvements in the structure of meetings; for example a division between strategic information seeking meetings and decision clarifying meetings.

- Collective learning by reflection.

The interplay between action structure and value structure

When you teach a technique or a method there is a great risk that the adepts are learning the steps mechanically, without chewing and assimilating them making them their own and without really understanding the meaning of them. The result can be empty gestures and hampering structures. Therefore, it is essential to take advantage of opportunities to practice the methods on issues that are close to everyday life and that the adepts find urgent to solve. When they have their focus on problem solving at work, they forget that they are involved in a learning process and start reflecting over what made it go so well. Then they can see the pattern and through their own experience understand the benefit of each step. They can take ownership over the method and use it in their own way, where they are of the best use.

Resistance to change is usually about the unwillingness to leave well-trained habits that we feel safe to use. Therefore, we can as well take the chance to widen the issue and use the situation as a case for practice every time when we anyway have to change something thoroughly to look for something new and untried. When the confusion is there anyway, we can use it to look for even more profound improvements.

The reason for confusion is our need of structures to be able to orient ourselves. So when habitual structures are dissolving, we have to try to find our way step by step by an interplay between a "value structure" (what we need and like in our interaction with the environment, what we want to preserve or want more or less of) and an "action structure" (what conditions and space for action the environment is offering us).

For example, if we find waiting too long and boring in ordinary hide and seek (value structure), we can change the action structure by putting a tin by the "home" and give the participants the chance to free all who are taken by kicking the tin away before the seeker is there. This will add some action and excitement to the game.

In a similar way, we can look for new, and until now untried, measures of progress and manners of interaction in our everyday life. For example, if the company for some reason has to change premises, we can at the same time take the chance to ask what we would have liked to do (value structure), but were not given enough space or was too complicated in the old premises (action structure). In what way could new premises give better conditions for what we have been longing for (action structure + value structure)? In a similar way we can ask what obstacles would disappear through the use of new technology and what new opportunities it could bring. Or an organisational change, a new information system or any kind of a planned change.

It is important to give people a chance to mourn what they experience as lost by a change at hand in order to give them an opportunity to say goodbye and thank you to the old. After that they may be ready to welcome the new. If you do this carefully in real dialogue, where all can be heard in a constructive way, you also get a good picture of what value structure is prevailing in the company. At the same time, those involved can get some support in focusing on what new attractive untried things the new can bring, if it is helped to become reality. Again this will give opportunities for practicing I-Thou-contact in the real world where it is most important. Here the support from consultants who are used to working with dialogues can be of significant value. It is experiences from real processes that give lasting results.

More examples where I-Thou-meeting is both goal and means

Interactions in the world are still dominated by hierarchies, where people act more on the basis of their role and place in the hierarchy than as responsible persons. It's not so different from the original culture in that group of baboons, but usually with other symbols of power than brutal violence. Therefore I get very touched and happy, as do so many others with me, when we see all the different examples of how much it is possible to achieve by more I-Thou contact:

Class 9A. A team of teachers who were universally recognised as especially competent accepted the challenge of supporting a class of about twenty fifteen year old pupils in a low achieving school to become one of the three best classes in the whole of Sweden in one year. Quite a challenge! And they succeeded! It was mostly thanks to an intensive I-Thou-interaction - with the pupils, with each other and the management of the school.

All this was followed by a TV documentary by the Swedish Television, SVT, in a series of programmes, where we came quite close to both teachers and pupils. The personal touch caught a large audience and made a profound impression on viewers in different ages. My fifteen-year-old grandson followed the programs with the same fascination as my forty-year-old son and myself, seventy.

The teachers took their mission seriously. Their first challenge was to get the pupils on board and overcome their suspicions to accept their support. They needed to become convinced that there was meaning for them in improving at school other than pleasing the teachers and proving their competence, or having the objective of making money and the like. The beginning was very much about getting away from the suspected I-It-relationship and creating an I-Thou-relationship. It involved relationships based on honest, straightforward and mutual communication where it is as important to listen to and support the pupils to express their needs, as it is to communicate and be heard in their own experiences and opinions.

One reason for the success was probably the teachers´ passion for their respective subjects. But the most salient feature among the teachers who became the special heroes in the documentary was their obvious and genuine interest in each pupil. Each pupil was addressed as a person on their own. Disappointments and irritations were expressed with the same clarity as joy over successes of different kinds. The commitment was not only expressed in words, but also in action. For example, house calls (without criticising forefingers), to accompany a shy girl on her way to school, experimenting with digestible pieces (instead of all or nothing), or where the music teacher gave a talented pupil his old bass guitar. The teachers were not only interested in results, but also in the ways the pupils were wrestling with their lives, attempting to be true to themselves and others, to choose, etc. For example, the physical training teacher was also a yoga teacher, and the Swedish teacher also led dialogues about views on life. The pupil and her knowledge and ambitions were put into its greater context.

The teachers also had to wrestle with their own failures and the temptation to give up. When half of the available time had passed, they began to believe that they had promised too much and wanted to subdue the demands. They had really tried and were tired, and the pupils were too much behind from the beginning. This reflected badly on the two headmasters who had risked their reputation in starting this project and who had suffered quite a lot of mockery for their vain hopes. They expressed their disappointment and fear of the consequences of failure quite clearly. This made the teachers mobilise new hope and find new energy and they succeeded in their seemingly hopeless enterprise.

What had started as an ego-boosting challenge to show one's competence, ended in a moving story of humanity, engagement, interplay between different personalities, closeness - yes, love. About the importance of being seen and respected in one´s distinctive character. Mutuality. I-Thou. Or as one of the teachers described it, "At first I met twenty pupils. Now I leave twenty friends." At the breaking-up not one eye was tearless neither among the involved teachers and pupils nor among the TV viewers. This is something that we all understand and long for - genuine contact.

Gareth Malone, a young British choirmaster (born 1975), practiced a similar approach with empathic I-Thou-contact and enthusiasm in his attempts to recruit and train singers in the most unlikely settings. He succeeded in awakening the interest at a school for juvenile delinquents and carried out a well reviewed concerto. He started choirs in South Oxhey, a society with no cultural traditions whatsoever of that sort. He stimulated ten-year-old boys to radically improve in mathematics, reading and writing. All this and maybe more is documented in a number of TV documentaries. So rather than writing about him, I warmly recommend you to look him up on the internet.

Carolina Klüft was a heptathlon world champion for many years and there were no signs that she would stop winning. She got rich and famous. But while most of us are running around like hell, dreaming about more, more, watch me, see me, higher salary, finer titles, more expensive cars ... she, a twenty-five-year-old woman stopped her successful and ego-boosting competition, saying to herself, "Now wait ... is this fun any more? Am I learning anything new? Is it worth it?"

When she was interviewed about why she was leaving her very successful sport to specialise in long jump where she was more mediocre, she replied:
- It is easy to be too influenced by the opinions of others and I don´t want to submit to achievement hysteria.
- Here and now is what is valid for me. I want to live my life.
- Now I follow my own philosophy, to feel joy, have fun and get new experiences.
- I have had a dialogue with myself, looked for different signs and followed my heart.
- I go for something new and that is very reckless, I know, but it feels so right and inspiring.

If we are brave enough, all of us have the chance to do as Carolina, to leave our safe and successful comfort zones and follow our hearts into new, challenging and inspiring fields where there can be more passion in our lives. Or to create more space for qualities that were sacrificed in habitual work. Take for example a well-known managing director, who had been CEO in different companies for more than twenty years. He left his job because, "The world becomes too narrow and one-sided if all available time is devoted to reading economic reports". He wanted more time for his family, friends and his own interests, such as learning philosophy and cultivating his garden.

If you look around, you will probably notice many interesting examples of both the importance of I-Thou-contact and of how the energy goes where you put your focus.

An experienced interrogator has learnt that if you want to find the truth by a cross-examination of a suspect, you first have to see the human behind the criminal action and to be honest and open with yourself. It is about building a trustful relationship, without which the accused will never tell what really happened.

Which events make the most profound and lasting impressions on you? I believe that it is the personal stories that will stand out for you, where people share their personal experiences, their difficulties or passions in their lives or jobs from a scene in a TV or radio programme, or in a direct encounter with you. Where you can share the other´s perspective and recognise yourself one way or another and mirror yourself as a human being. And I believe that it is the I-Thou-quality of the dialogue that is touching you, where you feel kind of invited - in contrast to when you are experiencing a talking-about; I-It.

My son in law, Rille, has a painting-company. They were hired to renovate a housing area. One of the flats was inhabited by a woman who was so drug-addicted that she had lost custody of her children. Her drug friends came and went as they wanted and made it impossible for the painters to work there. Then Rille seized her and showed her a flat that they had recently renovated, "We want to make your flat as nice as this one. Do you want that?" Yes she did.

"But then we need to help each other. We cannot do our job as long as your friends are floating around like this," Rille said.

"But I can't keep them away", said the woman.

"OK, then we have to put in new locks. We can do that for you. Then you have to take care of the keys." So that was done. Her flat became painted and nice. And when the woman felt cared about and counted on, she straightened up and could live up to her new standard. She didn't play about in the area any more and Rille thought that she even got back custody of her children. Again I-Thou.

The book *The Necessary Revolution* by Peter Senge et al. (2008) offers a collection of examples of how much can be done, when you focus on a green technology. And new examples are coming up almost every day. They can be large scale initiatives, such as when South Korea went in for a green future technology. The government is running a green growth politics and the industry is concentrating on electrical cars, batteries, 3D-screens and wind-power, but also on new services. The drive behind this hunt for new growth motors is the competition from China, as well as the lack of domestic energy. So thoughts about what is needed for a transition to a sustainable development are not only coming from the West, but indeed also from the East. A small scale example of this is when the Grameen Bank, by their micro-loans and education in renewable energy production, began supporting poor Indian women to sell and install a solar energy package in villages in the countryside. Or offered equipment for transforming droppings from cows and chickens into biogas. This way the people in the villages can get much better energy at the same cost as the paraffin they used before.

Maybe the great is done in a small scale by the many. I have mentioned a couple of examples that make me happy and hopeful. Now that your awareness of transforming forces is awake, you will probably notice a lot more examples around you, in media and in your everyday life. The world is full of people who are both willing and able if they get the space to try.

The first step towards a realisation of all good intentions is probably just encouragement and nourishment. For example, by arranging meeting-places for I-Thou-contact, where we feel free to share our observations, experiences and dreams in a constructive way. You can find a couple of suggestions for how this can be done at work and within the frame of everyday life in this book. You can also find a few thoughts on what discriminates a constructive dialogue from a destructive win-lose argument. Then it is up to you, and your creativity and relationship networks, to start your nourishment groups.

The fear of change is probably mostly about the fear of cutting off one´s nose to spite one´s face and tearing away the structures and systems that hold society together and leave it in a chaotic mess. A fear that we will lose our personal foothold when structures that we finally have learnt to master are replaced by others that we have not get used to and may not even understand. But we don´t have to change it all at once. Maybe our material needs are best met by the prevailing structures and systems, by mass production for a world market. A part of the population will always be needed here, although it may be a shrinking part. It is the exchange of qualities apart from this that we probably need to organise in another way. Things that can enrich our lives and can be offered at a market by people who are specialised in just this. Special qualities that people are willing to pay for which make them suitable to base new professions on. It is in our looking for these new professions that we need much more of I-Thou-contact. And this is probably where most of the jobs will be created, in due time, at least in the Western world of today. We can use the free space that is available when our basic needs are assured.

In our history we have experienced at least as troublesome transitions as the one awaiting us. My grandparents had an estate where I spent my summers. When I was a kid, the farm had its own smithy. Twelve horses and thirty-five men worked with the agriculture and had their own tool shed. When the farm was expropriated, and I was about twenty years old, two men with two tractors and big machines took care of the agriculture (except cows and garden). The whole country had the same transformation from an agricultural to an industrial society and from there further into the information and knowledge societies. For sure, a couple of qualities got lost in the transformation and some new ones were gained, but the transformation was relatively painless, at least when seen from this perspective after the fact.

So I am quite optimistic about our abilities to manage the transformation to sustainable development. Maybe we will even be able to use the confusion in the creative void between the old and the emerging new to create a desired future with surprising improvements of the quality of life that we didn´t know existed.

Everything begins with yourself. Who you are. How you want to live your life. What kind of world and future you want to contribute to. How you choose. Where you find your own nourishment and inspiration. What responsibility and what initiatives you are willing to take.

Epilogue

The consciousness needed for a transformation of the world is rapidly rising. During the year since I wrote the Swedish version of this book, so much has happened that I have had to re-write and add several passages when translating it into English. A clearer worldview is emerging, at least among those people who are concerned about a sustainable future.

Recently, I participated in the symposium *Co-create the Future*, arranged by the network Awakening the Dreamer (www.awakeningthedreamer.org and www.pachamama.org). From there I heard a very lively description of the challenges we are facing in the world today, what has brought us to this point and what steps we could take towards sustainable development. Using visualisations and other techniques helped us to digest the impressions, making them our own. It was an excellent symposium. It is held in a number of venues worldwide and I recommend it to everyone. Making a single day's investment to obtain this level of understanding is a small cost for our shared future.

My first reaction was that my book is superfluous and unnecessary! My message is spread much better in the way that the symposium did, by video and dialogue. But then I realised that one reason why they could present such a rich picture was that many people had spoken their truth from their different points of view and the people from Awakening the Dreamer had put it together into a meaningful whole. The same thing described from different angles and in different words creates a better understanding. And expressing your truth in your way is personally instructive and joyful to yourself, even if nothing new is said. The change from your end starts by you understanding your inner world so that you can change the outer one!

The most important thing for me in writing this book was to collect all the loose ends in my thoughts about sustainable development and put them together into a meaningful and coherent whole. And what I found out gave me hope, because the transformation process that is forced upon us by climate change and the like contains many of the qualities and skills that I believe will be important parts of the necessary new measures of progress and goals. The means become the goals.

But of course I want the book to be of some value for you as a reader as well. I hope that you will be able to see yourself in it and recognise parts of your own thinking as well as find some support in collecting your own loose ends into a whole that feels meaningful to you where you stand in your life. I hope that you become able to see your life in its greater context and gain the inspiration to contribute towards a sustainable future in your own special way.

So let's continue to expand our knowledge and express our true selves!

Network and nourishment groups

A transformation like this is a long-term process that needs to be taken step by step. Seemingly nothing happens until a critical mass of people from different places in the society is in favour of such a dramatic change. Therefore, it is difficult to keep the engagement alive alone. As encouragement, some people may be longing for support and help in their own personal development or a change in their own work. Others are longing for a place where they can freely express their engagement and hope for some response. A lot is happening in the direction that I have put forward in this book. There are lots of opportunities, but as a starting point in your search I hereby give you a few examples of organisations and networks that are on the same track as myself.

Some organisations for a sustainable development:

Awakening the Dreamer: www.awakeningthedreamer.org

Higher ambition: www.higherambition.org

Light Spira: www.lightspira.org

New Era Net: www.neweranet.org

Pachamama Alliance: www.pachamama.org

Pragati Leadership: www.pragatileadership.com

Society for organisational learning, SoL: www.solonline.org

Social Venture Network, SVN: www.svn.org
The Equality Trust: www.equalitytrust.org.uk
The Natural Step: www.thenaturalstep.org
Tällberg Foundation: www.tallbergfoundation.org

Gestalt in organisations:
There are consultants and Gestalt therapists all over the world. You will probably be able to find them where you are.

Reference literature

Beer, Michael & Fredberg, Tobias et al (2011): *Higher Ambition – how great leaders create economic and social value.* Harvard Business Review Press

Collins, Jim (2001): *Good to Great.* HarperCollins Publishers NY

Covey, Stephen R (2006): *The 8:th Habit.* FranklinCovey Co

Csikszentmihalyi, Mihalyi (1990): *Flow.* Harper Perennial, NY

Damasio, Antonio (1999): The Feelig of What Happens.

Damasio, Antonio (2003): *Looking for Spinoza*

Goleman, Daniel & Senge, Peter (2007): *Working with Presence.* CD-book Audio Renaisance, NY

Jenkins, Ralph & Örnesved, Marie: (2010): *Sensitelligent.* Matador

Katie, Byron (2002): *Loving What Is*

Kenyon, Tom & Sion, Judi (2002): *The Magdalen Manuscript.* Sounds True Inc

Rock, David & Schwartz, Jeffrey (2007): *The Neuroscience in Leadership.* The Journal of Strength-based Interventions, no 3, USA

Senge, Peter et al (2005): *Presence.* Nicholas Brealy Publ.

Senge, Peter et al (2008): *The Necessary Revolution.* Doubleday

Tolle, Eckhart (2005): *A New Earth.* Dutton Adult

Tronick, Ed (2007): The Neurobehavioral and Socio-Emotional Development of Infants and Children. Norton, NY

Wilkinson, Richard & Pickett, Kate (2009): *The Spirit Level – Why Equality is Better for Everyone.* Penguin Books, London

Yontef, Gary (1993): *Awareness, Dialogue & Process.* The Gestalt Journal Press Inc, NY

making **messages** from
loving hearts
available to a **global** audience

cocreators @lightspira.com
www.lightspira.com

www.ingramcontent.com/pod-product-compliance
Lightning Source LLC
Chambersburg PA
CBHW031156020426
42333CB00013B/698